Book IV

Whispers, Tears, Prayers & Hope

Poetry and Song Lyrics By

Ed Roberts

So much has happened since I left the pen
Setting on the table
So much has changed
So much has remained the same

In two years
So many words have found their way to paper
So many others have slipped by
Refusing to be captured

Finally the time has come
The time to gather the crops from the field
Sort the pages
And leave them here
For you to read

Today the world stands in need of so many things
My simple prayer
Is that you might find at least a little of what you
seek
Here among the pages of my life

At the back of this book I have left a special poem
"Ink in the Storm." Many people ask me why I
choose to write poetry. I think this poem will help you
understand the answer to this question. I do not do
this for myself; I do it for them.

Table of Contents

Whispers, Tears, Prayers, and Hope

A school bell rings in Dafur.
Children gather for their daily dose of hope.
They know that simply by being there
They put their lives in danger.
Still they sit,
Listen carefully to each lesson,
And train themselves
To be the future of their people
Because they know
How many lives were sacrificed
How much blood was spilled
To give them this opportunity.

A frail man stands in line
Just like he did yesterday.
He will wait hours
Simply to receive a small bag of rice
And a few precious bottles of water.
He will take these blessed gifts
Home to his family
And like yesterday
Save very little for himself.
Still he smiles
Because he knows
They will all survive
Another day.

A woman slowly packs her clothes
Into the small suitcase upon her bed.
She gathers her two children
And silently slips out the door
Trying her best
Not to make a sound

Afraid she will wake him.
The three end up in a strange new place
Filled with others
That are fleeing the same conditions.
She knows the next few months will be tough
But now deep down
She knows now at least they stand a chance.

I sit here at my computer
With tears running down my face
And try to capture just a few words.
Words that might serve as a simple reminder
Of the many blessings we all have in our lives.
Words left here to remind us
That there still is so much for us to give.
The most important of which
Is hope.

These are words that flow so freely.
Each like a single teardrop
That falls upon this keyboard.
Each one of them a whisper.
Each one
A simple prayer.

Ed Roberts 12/15/05

Storms

Storms
There are always storms
Lightning flashes
Thunder crashes
The winds roar
They attack us at our very core
Then
Of course
The rain comes

The rain falls all around us
Blinds us
Soaks us until nothing is left dry
It batters all that we hold precious
Seemingly relentless to bring about
Utter destruction

Storms
Yes, there are always storms
They wash things away
Often things we would rather hold on to
But as it is meant to be
In the end
The choice is not ours to make

In all of their power
All of their destruction
One thing is certain
All storms end

They leave
Often as quickly as they appear
They move on

They leave us
Sometimes broken
Sometimes shattered
Sometimes damaged beyond repair

We often are left
Standing amongst the rubble
Breathless
Exhausted
And facing many tough decisions

We can simply move on
Abandon what was once precious
Pack up what has been spared
And try to find new shelter
Often not having any idea where that might be

Or we can stop
Gather our belongings
Dispose of what can't be repaired
Fix what we are able
And rebuild on familiar ground

In either case
In the middle of the night
We are faced with but one certainty

Storms
There will always be
Storms

Ed Roberts 11/17/06

Fill in the _____ s

It's all the _____ s fault
They take our jobs
They rape our women
They kill our children
The _____ s have no remorse

All the _____ s are terrorist
They preach hatred
Pray to their own God for our destruction
They are even willing to kill themselves
Just for a chance to kill us

I hate the _____ s
You should too
They don't deserve to live
People here are starving
People here are dying
Because of them

It's all the _____ s fault
The world would be such a better place
Without them

Far too often this leads to
The _____ s are not even human
It really is okay to kill them

In the end
Nothing will ever change
Not as long as people keep filling in
These _____ 's

Ed Roberts 1/17/07

The Sound of Music

A mockingbird sings his own concerto
While crickets play harmony
To his tune
The wind rustles leaves at our feet
Whispering tales through branches
That hang above our heads
Music surrounds us all
Too often though
We drown it with our iPods
Settling instead
For noise

Ed Roberts 6/21/07

Signs

Why is it
That the first sign
So many people look for
Is the dollar sign

When I would rather
See signs of change
Instead

Ed Roberts 2/23/06

So many times the dollar changes nothing
Until it itself is broken into change.

Every Day Choices

The hungry are hungry
Every day
It is up to us
Whether or not
We choose to feed them

The homeless are homeless
Every day
It is up to us
Whether or not
We choose to shelter them

The sick are sick
The addicted are addicted
The dying are dying
Every day
It is up to us
Whether or not
We give them care

The church is there
Every day
It is up to us
Whether or not
We choose to go inside

Heaven is there
Every day
In so many ways
It is up to us
Whether or not
We will ever hope to share its glory

"For I was an hungered
And ye gave me meat
I was thirsty
And ye gave me drink
I was a stranger
And ye took me in
Naked
And ye clothed me
I was sick
And ye visited me
I was thirsty
And ye gave me drink
I was a stranger
And ye took me in

Inasmuch as ye have done it
Unto one of the least of these
My brethren
Ye have done it
Unto me" *

* taken from St. Matthew 26 King James Version
of the Bible

The Phoenix Diane

Done
Finished
Over
A wasted life ended
With a 22 caliber shot to the head
Just in case
The slashes on the wrists
Don't end this worthless life
Soon enough

A heap of drug-filled
Alcohol-soaked flesh
Left to rot away
In a pool of ever-growing crimson
A life worth less now
Than when it first began

Flashing lights
Hands upon hands
Reaching out
Pulling
Scraping
Working with broken flesh
Pulling it back together
More blood they scream
More blood they give

Blackness comes

Birth
Beginning
Resurrection

Light not at the end of the tunnel
But from within
Hope
Compassion
Unequaled love from a stranger

I am new once more
With meaning
Purpose
Not yet fully understood

Not at all deserved
But nonetheless given
To me

Student of life
Teacher to those who will listen
Friend to those in need
All of these now
I have become

A new life given
This time
Shall not be wasted

A new beginning
Priceless beyond comprehension

A woman
Yet a child
In so many ways
With innocence regained

Ed Roberts 7/09/07
(Based on a true story)

Collateral

You call this a war zone
You send men with guns
From far away
Men that are fighting for some cause
Some purpose
In which
They truly believe

You make this a battlefield
Guns in every arm
IED's on the street
No one here is safe

You call this
Hell

This is not a battlefield
This is not a war zone
This is only Hell
Because you have made it this way

This is my home

I was born here
Was raised here
I used to work here
Before the shops closed down
Before those that could
Left

Yes
I would take my family
From this place

Leave this city
If I could
But who is to say
That you would not follow
Is there really a place
That you would not go?

Where am I to hide my children
How can I
Feed them
Educate them
Most important
Keep them safe?

They play among the gunfire
Collect shell casings
For toys
And souvenirs to sell
They eat from garbage cans
And beg for food when they can

You ask me why I am angry
Why I yell and scream
At all who will listen

Inside
I am still the same man
A simple shop keeper
My pride
You have stripped from me
You wash your boots
Everyday
With my soul

I care not
Who wins
Or loses
I care not
How many of you must die

In the end
All I care about
Is when the fighting will be over

Then
And only then
Can I raise my family in peace

Ed Roberts 7/15/06

When there's nothing else

When you smile your tender smile
I smile inside and out
When you shed a single tear
I cry an ocean
No matter what it's all about

When your world shatters
I pick up the pieces
One by one
Help you put them back together
Until you're whole again

When there's nothing left that I can say
I don't let words get in our way

When there's nothing else that I can do
I just love you

Ed Roberts 10/01/07

21

Blue Eyes

You were once someone's pet
Groomed
Well fed
Cared for
Loved

I often wonder
What happened
What cast you to this fate

I saw you first
At my doorstep
Your coat still possessed
That cared-for shine
You were so beautiful
A full-blood Himalayan
Not a cat one would expect
To find wandering the street

You asked me for food
With such a gentle voice
You rubbed across my pants leg
Just in case
I couldn't hear

I couldn't say no
But I guess you already knew that
Cats are really so much smarter than we are

My wife even put a cat bed
On the porch for you
Even though she knew
This was only a place for you to visit

The street had now become your home
I would sometimes sit and watch you
Through the window
As you lay hiding in the grass
Waiting to pounce
On a bird or squirrel
That got too close

I never saw you actually kill anything
Though I did often find
An occasional tail
Or feathers that you left

I never tried to pet you
I know you are a tomcat
I have seen your battle scars
Often heard you
As you fought to maintain your turf

You are such a magnificent animal
With those ocean blue eyes
That can speak directly to one's soul

Two days ago
Letha found another cat
One that you had taken to be your mate

She was on the front porch
Near death
But I am afraid
Not close enough

When I first saw her
My heart wept
Filled my eyes
With more tears than they could hold

I was also filled with fear
For I have seen the signs of this sickness before

One only has to see the signs of rabies once
They are forever burned into your memory
After that

Without touching her
I was able to get her into a box
I wanted so much
Just to hold her
Stroke her coat
Let her know
She was still loved
But I knew a simple scratch could be fatal
I held the box instead

We took her to the shelter
They said they might test her
But then again
They may not

Cats are such low priority
Dogs are their greatest worry

Still they gave us a trap
A small cage to bring home

We know that you were next to her
Slept beside her on the porch

I also can see that something
Has scratched you
Left gashes behind your ear

I sit here tonight
Typing words
Or trying to
Through my tears
For I know the trap is in the yard
Waiting
It is waiting there
For you

I know if I catch you
I will have to take you to them
My fairest Blue Eyes
And I wish I could lie to myself
And tell myself they will try and find a way
To help you
Try to find a new warm place for you to stay
But I have never been good
At lying
Especially to my own heart

I know that if you are infected
Even a small scratch or nip
Could lead to my death
Or to the death of another
But tonight I sit here typing
And praying
That somehow in the morning
I find nothing
But an empty cage

If you are there tomorrow
I hope somehow God
Will find a way to forgive me
For what I have to do.

Ed Roberts 4/25/06

25

Tears of a Monster

Today
I was the monster

I captured a cat
One that I cared for
Loved more than even I knew
In a cage
On my front porch

I delivered that cat to people
People that I know
Most certainly
Will send it
To its death

Most people who see this cat
See a battered animal
A stray
A threat to their own livelihood

I see an animal
That used to be someone's pet
Used to be loved
Cared for
A Himalayan
With the most beautiful blue eyes
That could reach deep inside you
And touch your very soul

I delivered Blue Eyes
To them today
For your safety
And mine

For our sake
I became the monster
That we needed me to be

Tonight I sit here weeping
Not only for the loss
Of an animal that I held so dear
I weep for those
That I handed him over to
For it is their job to clean up
After all of our mistakes

Most of all
Though
I weep for us
You and me
For each of us carries a portion
Of the blame for this sin

People take in animals
Because they want them
Feel they need them
But way too often
In the end
Discard them
To try and fend for themselves

Today
I became your monster
A deliverer of death
To an animal I truly loved
A lot more than you can imagine

Judge me if you wish
But understand
I have already condemned myself

Yes
I stand before you
Guilty as charged

I just pray that you
And most important
God
Understand
Why it is
That tonight
This monster
Cries

Ed Roberts 4/27/06

The Silent Dance

To the howling of the wind
In the middle of the night I awaken
I lay here beside you
Ever so still, ever so quiet
And drink in each moonbeam
That bounces off of your subtle figure
I silently count each of your breaths
You let out a gentle moan
And in your sleep
You turn and place your arm across my body
Through it
I can feel each beat of your heart
My breathing quickens
As my pulse rises
Inches away lies pleasure
What my body so longs to touch
My mind screams out
through the building hunger
In three more hours
Your alarm will sound
In four you have to be at work
I close my eyes
In my mind our bodies become one
We share each breath
My heart beats in
Yours beats out
The storm subsides into a gentle sleep
As once again
Our souls dance through a not so quiet night
The silent dance
Of Love

Ed Roberts 2/13/07
(To Letha with Love)

Wings of an Angel

It's Ten PM
I turn to her
Give her a gentle kiss on the lips
And in a soft voice
Wish her "sweet dreams"

I lay there
Quietly
Motionless
Watch the moonlight
As it slowly bathes her
In its gentle radiance

It doesn't take long
Mere moments
Before you can see them
Spreading slowly from her shoulders
Covered in feathers
Dipped in moonbeams
Every night
She quietly spreads
Her silver wings

When I am finally sure she lies there
Sleeping
I slip from beneath the covers
Carefully creep to the dresser
And as quiet as I can
Remove the scissors from my drawer

One by one
I clip them
Silver feathers

That silently fall to the floor of our bedroom

Each morning
With the hint of the dawn
They disappear
Wisps or mere memories
Leaving not a single trace

Yes
Each night
I clip the wings of an angel
Hold her here
Earthbound
For just another day

I know the day is coming
When God will finally take her
The feathers come back
So much quicker than they did before

I hope He understands
And when my time comes
He is forgiving
And if not
To me it doesn't matter
To keep us together
For but a few more hours
In the end
I would gladly trade my wings in
For hers

Ed Roberts 7/04/06

Stairway to Heaven

In this world of darkness
I exist
Four walls surround me
Concrete both above
And below

Safe
I am here
Knowing every inch
Of my small world

At the edge of my existence
Hidden in the shadows
There stands a flight of stairs
Rotting slowly away
Like me
A victim of time

I have spent many days
Sitting at their base
Wondering where it is
That they may lead

Many a time
Have I placed my foot
Upon the first step
Unsure of where they lead
I stop

Would they take me
To my freedom
A world far beyond imagination
Or would they lead to my destruction

To a hell far worse than this
In time
I know they like myself
Will fall to ruin
Become so much ash
Upon this concrete floor
I know not
Which of us
Will go first
One day
I hope I find the courage
Am able to overcome fear itself
And upon these steps
I will finally climb

Each night I pray
Tomorrow will be this day

Ed Roberts 1/24/08

I wrote this for a woman at work who had been in an abusive relationship for almost ten years. She told me this poem helped her decide to leave him in Oklahoma and return to Texas to be closer to her family.
Sometimes we must decide to take the stairs, whether or not we know where they lead.

The Brush

On the dresser
There rests a brush
The handle is chipped and faded
Its shine long gone
From use

My hair is nearly gone
What is left
Has faded to white
I really have no use for a brush
One look in my direction
And of this
You will be very sure

But each morning I wake
And stare at it
This brush on my dresser
Some nights
I pick it up examine it closely
And hold it
First to my nose
And then
Sit quietly in bed
Holding it close to my heart

You see
I can tell you
Just how many hairs there are
Tangled amongst those fine white bristles
Twenty-four to be precise

And even though it has been two years
Since my Ruby has left my side
The brush still smells
Of her

Each night
Before I finally surrender to sleep
I place the brush
Ever so carefully
Back in the special spot on the dresser
Where she kept it
So she could find it
Even without the lights
Because
The first thing she did every morning
Was to hum ever so softly
While she brushed her ruby red hair

No
One good look in my direction
And you can be certain
That I'll never use this brush again
But if you stop for a moment
Look closer to count my tears
You'll understand
Why I need this brush so much

Every night I lay here
Alone in the darkness
Praying that when I do finally awaken
From what little sleep my heart allows

That I won't spend another morning
Sitting on the edge of this king size bed
Waiting a few precious moments
In the soft morning light
Staring at a brush on the dresser
Hoping instead to hear
Her heavenly hum

Ed Roberts 5/08/06

(For Nanny)

A Lesson in Faith

They waited every Saturday
Until the sun had gone down
Until they were sure
There were no soldiers in the jungle
Watching

They gathered in a small clearing
Sometimes they would dare to light a small fire
Most of the time though
Their only light was that of the moon

They came in the rain
In the cold
And in the heat of summer
All came by foot
Sometimes carrying those
That could no longer walk

He was always the first into the jungle
And always the last to leave
With his very life
He protected them
For to him
These were his children
And to them
He was their Father
Their one and only priest

They all knew what would happen
If the soldiers found them there
Each and every one
Knew the price of their faith

Still into the jungle they went
Every Saturday night
To receive their own piece
Of the bread of life
And to listen to him read
From the Bible that he kept hidden
In a small altar made of stone

Without fail
Every Sunday morning
The soldiers came

He would stand there waiting for them
In the center of the village
Alone

Sometimes they would yell at him
First
Other times they simply began their task
Without a word
They would beat him with their rifles
Kick his body
When he fell to the ground
Laugh at him
Because he offered no resistance
And stopped
Only when they had tired from the ordeal

Every Sunday
He stood there and waited for them
For he knew if he was not there
Another would take his place

Secretly
Each of soldiers admired him
And yes
In many ways
Feared him as well
For they knew so many eyes were watching
And forgiveness was one thing
They would never take by force

For so many years
He stayed in this small village
Helping those that could to leave
Helping those that could not
To survive

The day came though
He could stay with them no longer
His very presence there
Was too great of a danger to them all

The Church made the final arrangements
Took him from his homeland
And finally
After many secret refuges
Ended up
Bringing him into mine

I did not know him
As well as I wanted to
And needed to
But in him
I could see the true meaning
Of the words faith and hope

I look at all the churches here in my hometown
(There are over 20 pages of churches alone in the
phone book)
And wonder
How many of these would be filled
If there were soldiers in our streets
How many would be there
Even under the cloak of darkness
As well
In the short time
That I knew this special man
That God had given us
To serve as a reminder of the true power of faith
I learned so many things

One of which
Is to question the very depth
Of my own

Ed Roberts 1/30/06

Dedicated to Father Bao
A true angel among men

Cardio Poetic Resuscitation

Clear

"There was a man
Who left a bar
He didn't have too much to drink
Or so he thought"

A young couple reads a poem online
After which they decide to clear out their liquor
cabinet
They decide they never want to be able to truly
understand this poem
Ever

Clear

"My future I leave here along with what's left of my
heart
Hopefully to give company
To the innocence that was taken
And put here by me

They might someday forgive me
God may find a way to forgive me
But here I stand
Just a reflection of a man
For I know the day will never come
The day that I
Can forgive Myself"

A man lies in a hospital bed
He cries after reading a poem
He knows the body that he placed in the ground

Was that of his son
He vows to spend the rest of his life
Trying to keep others from becoming
The man who left the bar
Clear

"I jab the needle deeper
Trying to kill the last bit of soul that remains
A few hours bought at such a price
Knowing
Tomorrow the reflection will return again
Deep down
Praying it will all end
Before I once more remember
Who it was
I used to be

No
Mustn't let go
Must hang on
You can be me again

They
Still
Love
You"

A young man sitting in front of a computer at a
library
Finds a poetry site by chance
He reads a poem
That he somehow feels
Was written especially for him
He decides to go back to his family
And try to be their son again

Clear

"He heard a whisper
A voice
Barely audible
But familiar somehow
Five words
That was it
Nineteen letters
That made him stop

Who will find your body?"

A woman
Searching the internet
Desperate to find some reason
Not to do what she has decided to do
Finds a poem
And decides
To put the bullet in her jewelry box on her dresser
Instead of into her head

Clear

"The daughter turns up the radio again
Turns on her computer
And chats with her "friends"
People she has never met before
And tries not to look at her leg
Tries not to think of the razor blade
That she hides in her dresser
Tries not to cut herself again
She has all of these things in her life
A nice house
All the new clothes
The best television

The best computer money can buy
But still there is something missing
She picks up the blade
Just to make sure
That she is still alive"

A young girl
Receives a poem in her e-mail
She decides to put away her razor blades
Find out what is missing in her life
And starts to write poetry
For the first time in her life

Clear

No, Death
You can not have them

"Not as long as these lips have words to form
Or there are tales to be spun
From these withered hands
For as much as I am
This is truly
ME"

Clear

Ed Roberts 5/3/07

Pain

Pain
It's all around us

From the first breath we take
Our life is filled with pain

From our first fall
Our first scrape
We learn hot
We learn cold
We learn how important the word "No" can be
All of this
We learn by pain

It is part of us
It protects us
It destroys us
It lets us know we are alive
It kills us ever so slowly

From the day to day wear and tear
Our body heals
Pain is merely part of the process
It tells us when to stop
Warns us when we've gone too far

It can be our friend
It can be
Our worst enemy

We try and wash it away
Even with our first tear
We pray to be delivered from it

At the same time
We hold it close to our heart
Dig it up
When we want it the least
Are haunted by it
From the very core of our heart

Pain
It is all around us
Waiting to make us stronger
Waiting to bring us to our knees

In our lives
It can have so many faces
So many different levels
The toughest of which
We often inflict
Needlessly
Upon ourselves

Ed Roberts 10/24/06

Thou shalt not steal

Stealing is a sin

If a person steals from you
Out of greed
The sin is theirs

If a person steals from you
Out of need
The sin is yours
Because you made them

Ed Roberts 3/19/07

Work

I woke up one morning
My job was gone
I had seen it coming
Though honestly
I had tried hard not to look
This had happened before
I had sworn I'd be ready
I had sworn to keep more money in the savings
Sworn to pay off those credit cards
Yep, I had sworn all of those things
That morning
I did some swearing as well

You see
It's just something you start to take for granted
Those paychecks start coming
You bitch and moan
Complain about how crappy your job is
But deep inside
There's this little voice that reminds you
Hey stupid at least you still gotta job

Back to this morning
The one I woke up to

I pulled out my wallet
Twenty three dollars
Yep, that was what was there
I thought about the fifty I had blown
Spent the day before on VCR tapes
Yes, I had a lot of them
Almost 800 at that time
I looked at those

Thought of how much could have
Should have been dollars in the bank instead
Hence the little more swearing that morning

You know what though
I still woke up that morning
Dusted off an old copy of my resume
Added the latest job information
And hit the streets

Yes, it took about a week
No, I didn't find exactly what I was looking for
But by the grace of God
I did find something

One day
I dream of being a writer
One day
I dream of actually being able to feed my wife and
me
With my pen
So far this is still a dream
One that I know may never come true

At least for now
Those paychecks are still coming
Yes, I occasionally catch myself complaining about
my job
But that voice inside is never as soft as it used to be
And there is always an extra hundred dollar bill
Hidden in my wallet
Just in case
Just in case tomorrow I have to wake up
And start this poem all over again

Ed Roberts 1/08/07

Your Last Tear

I am the very last tear
That you will shed
While upon this Earth

Will I be born
From joy
Sorrow
Or pain

Will you spend me
For a friend
For one that you care for
Or
Someone you love

Worse of all
Will I be born
From pity
And be shed for no one

No one
Except
Yourself

Ed Roberts 4/03/06

A Note to the Professor

I come here to your classroom
Your student
I sacrifice my money
Money that did not come easily
To trade here for your time

Before you start
I have but a few questions

What is it
You are here to teach
When our short time here is over
What is it that I will walk away with
That I did not have before

What is it you will give me
That I could not obtain
On my own

No
I am not asking for you to provide answers to me
I am but a simple student
I do know my place

I would hope though
Before I spend my money
And we both sit here
And spend our time
That you can at least provide answers
Answers to these few questions
If to no one else
But to yourself

Ed Roberts 10/31/06

51

Darkness

The church is just a building
Filled with a few sheep
Sworn to hold on
To lies

The wine is just wine
The bread is just bread
Nothing more

There is no Heaven
That awaits you
No Hell
For you to avoid

You
Yourself
Are simply bones and flesh
Some form of accident
A walking piece of meat
With a brain

The world is full
Of predators
And prey
The powerful
And the weak

If you are lucky
You just might be able to stand
In the small space
That lies between

There is no love
Only lust
No friendship
Only convenient acquaintances
When someone becomes of no use to you
You cast them aside
To find someone else

And in your darkest hour
When you stand at the very edge
Of the ultimate inevitable
There is no one to call out to

Your last pleading words
Will fall upon an empty space

You said you wanted a world without God
Here it is

Have a nice day

Ed Roberts 6/23/06

We all need Someone

We all need someone

Someone that we can call
When we really have nothing to say
Someone we can share our triumphs with
Even if they are "little" ones
Someone we share our defeats with
Even if the rest of the world doesn't seem to give a
damn

We all need someone
Someone we can call out to
When the shadows are closing in
When we are left stranded
Alone sitting on the highway of life
We all need someone
Someone we know who will pick us up

We all need someone
Someone who would drive through a rainstorm
Just to bring us an umbrella
Or just offer a strong shoulder to cry on
Or a hand to hold
When everything seems to be slipping away

We all need someone
Someone that will listen
And not be afraid to speak up
Even though they know
We probably won't listen to a thing they have to say

We all need someone
Someone to share our laughs

Dry our tears
Someone who in the end
Really needs us there as well
As for me
I was very lucky to find that someone
Luckier still
I married her

And she doesn't seem to mind
There are so many other "someones"
Out there as well.

Ed Roberts 11/18/06

Used Bride

Bride
As is
High mileage
Definitely not in new condition
No warranty implied
No returns
Given to groom
In same condition as above
With love

Ed Roberts 6/12/07

Someone at the End of the Day

An empty house
So many empty rooms
Empty days
Made up of so many empty hours
Some may look at it this way
Growing old

But a house has doors that can be opened
Empty rooms can easily become cluttered
And empty days or hours
Can be filled with precious moments

Sometimes whether people think
It is right or wrong does not matter
In life
Too soon is often far better than too late

At the end of even the shortest of days
We all need someone
That someone special
Who will be there just for us
Even if all we need
Is for them to be there
At the end of each day
To be that someone
Willing to turn off the light

Ed Roberts 6/12/07

(For Mom and A.C.)

Painless

Would you have me remove your pain
Take away the burning in your soul
Leaving nothing but cold regret
Cold lips
Yearning for a single kiss
Cold hands
Longing for a simple touch
A cold heart
Beating alone in an empty chest

Would you have me dry each tear
Silence each sob
Leave nothing but a shifting breeze
Cover each memory with so much dust

If I could remove your pain
Could you
Would you
Live with what remains

Ed Roberts 1/24/07

Angel at 17

He was 17
Just a normal kid
Well
Not really

He had seen so much
Done so much
Some things good
Some things bad
I guess most of us have by this time

Like me
He never seemed to fit in anywhere
He was either
Too fat
Too smart
Or simply too much

No, he wasn't into sports
And he had so much trouble with his grades
He wasn't as lucky as I was
But he worked so much harder
To get the grades that he did get
It seemed he worked hard at everything
And he had so many plans

He knew what he wanted to do after school
He had already met the girl of his dreams
They were going to spend their lives together
Together learning what life could be
They had already started a family
Though no one knew but them at the time
He was growing up so quickly

We were doing that together
That's what Best Friends do

Everything was going great
Until that night
When I got the phone call

There had been an accident
Yeah right
A single shot from his own gun
In his own apartment
And suddenly
For him it was over

The gun accidentally went off
They were just fooling around
That's what his "friend" told them
And of course
The police believed that

Dennis
The hole that was made
The day that you left
I know will never be filled

I carried you to the graveyard
And held your mother as she cried
She never did understand
Why it was her son that had to leave
I guess none of us did
And probably never will

I sometimes sit here and wonder
If somewhere in this world
Your son or daughter is out there
And hopefully you are there as well
To watch them
As only an angel can do

Ed Roberts 8/4/06

For Dennis

The Harvest

You plant seeds of hatred
Yet weep
When your harvest
Is nothing but blood and death

Your children are starving
Because they can not eat bullets

True power
Should not be measured
In how many lives you can destroy

Power comes from how many
You can save
Or change

A war can be started with but a single bullet
It can also be ended
With but a single act of compassion

Every day that we awake
We are faced with a litany of choice

Today
In the name of God
Choose peace

Ed Roberts 10/02/07

Beat Me

So
You think it makes you a man
To hit someone else with your hands

Ok
Beat me

I saw the marks that you left
On my sister
Yesterday
I counted her bruises
And what hurt me more
Is when she finally told me
You had done worse to her
Before

Ok now
Beat me

So
You gotta hit somebody
To prove you're a man
I'm give'n you your chance

Boy
Here I am
Beat me

I walk with a cane
You can see I can't run
Come on now
You can have yourself
Just a boatload of fun

Now
Beat me

There's one thing I gotta tell you
Just so you understand this real clear
You walkin' piece of dirt

I beat back!

Come on, now

Beat me

Ed Roberts 3/23/06

If they were coming for You

If they were coming for you
And you knew
Would you pack your things
And run

If they were coming for you
And you knew
Would you try and find some place to hide

If they were coming for you
And you knew
Would you gather your weapons
And fight

If they were coming for you
And you knew
Would you try and reason with them
Try to talk your way out

If they were coming for you
And you knew
You knew what it is
They would do

You knew you would be tortured
In the end
You knew that you would die a horrible death
But you knew
Your death would inspire thousands
Maybe millions

If they were coming for you
And you knew
You knew it all

What
Would
You
Do

Can any of us really be sure

Ed Roberts 6/02/07

The value of a painting

What gives a painting its value
Is it the paint
The colors
Does it have something to do
With what canvass on which it has been placed

Could it be
The number of brush strokes
The time it took its maker to finish

Is it the subject
What or who
The artist chose to capture

Does everything depend
On whose hand held the brush
Would two paintings of the same topic
Painted at the same time
By two different artist
Demand such a different price
Sometime in the future

What does give a painting its value
Who determines the price
How much money one must part with
To finally possess it

What makes it more
Than mere paint
Placed on canvass
By a single set of hands

Maybe if you have to stop and ask
This is something
You will never to be able to completely understand

In the end
This may be something
No one ever will

Ed Roberts 10/07/06

A Letter to Dad

I woke up this morning
Turned off the alarm clock
And got out of bed

Just like I used to do

I turned on the TV
Turned on the computer
And read my e-mails

Just another day

Later I ate lunch
Took a nap
Got back up
And got ready to go to work

Another ordinary day

I got home from work
Took a shower
Read a few more e-mails on the computer
And started off to bed

I had to stop
I couldn't walk past the paper and pen
That was sitting here on the desk
I couldn't walk past your picture
You know the one
The one hanging on the wall in the living room

No, everything today was normal
And probably will be tomorrow
Everything was just like it was before
But now you are gone

Dad
I could not imagine a world without you
Not having you there
Whenever I picked up the phone
When I found time for you
In all the everyday hustle of my life
Whenever I needed your support
Whenever I needed your help
You were always there
Dad

I'm the Grandfather now
The one that my sons turn to
When they find the time
When they are faced with their challenges
I'm the one that they call

God
I wish I was half as good at this
As you were

So tonight
I am sitting alone in a dark room
One on one
With paper and pen
Trying to capture these few words

Trying to write in between my tears
Just to let you know
The world isn't the same anymore
At least not for me
I know you're still here
Sometimes I can see your face
When I look at my sons
I can hear your laugh
Coming out of my grandson's mouth

Dad
I am writing this
Just to let you know
I am trying

Someday when we are back together again
You can let me know
Just how you think I did

Ed Roberts 1/27/07

Tumbling Walls

From a gentle slumber
Last night I was awakened
By a sound
My ears have waited a lifetime
To hear

Did you hear it
My friend

In the stillness of the night
The first wall
Fell

Today
I awoke

I went out into the world
Hammer in hand

There are far too many
Left standing

Together
We shall render them all
Into dust

Ed Roberts 9/12/06

Don't Call Me

Don't call me up at home
And tell me you went out
And got drunk last night
I don't want to know
I don't want to know why
How and especially
What happened afterward
Believe me
I can guess
Probably exactly what and why it happened
Last time

Believe me
I know about your demons
I understand your pain
Far better than most by the way
I do know how easy it can be
Simply to let it happen
Yes, I know a lot more than most
I also know about your wife
I know about your kids
I know each of them by name
What about them
Where were they
When you let it happen

We all have our pain we all have our demons
You are one of the very few
That know about mine
Do you think that somehow I'm not tempted
Do you think
The battle is easier for me
Somehow

I've told you why I don't go there
I've told you
Exactly what I fear it would cost
No, it's not a matter of if
It's only a matter of when
I've told you all of this before
And I'm telling you only once again

Next time
Don't call me
And tell me why you felt like
You had to go out and get drunk again

If you are going to call me, call me instead
When you feel like you need to
Or better yet
Why you wanted to but didn't
Call me about this anytime
Day or night

Just don't call me
When it's way too late
For me to help

If it's going to be then
Don't call me
At all

Ed Roberts 4/3/08

Sometimes we wait

A small group of people sit quietly
gathered so close together in a body,
yet so far apart from each other in mind.
Bill has been here now for fifteen days.
He does leave every now and then,
sometimes to run home to take a shower,
sometimes to grab a few hours of sleep.
But these visits to the outside world
are becoming shorter now and farther apart.
His mind and heart allow only some specific time
and distance before they pull him here,
back again, to sit and watch and wait.

Lucy came here yesterday.
Her face was soaked with tears.
Her whole body shook with fear.
She had been in a room such as this,
but never in circumstances like these.
She jumps at each new announcement,
paces the room every few minutes,
simply to calm her far too worn-out nerves.
Bill tries to comfort her; he knows this stage too well.
He also knows this is something
she will have to learn all by herself.

John came a few hours ago, his first time here,
though he has waited an eternity
for this special day to come.
He has talked about it, dreamed about it,
pictured it in, oh so many ways in his head.
Now that it is finally here, he is slowly starting to
realize this place has a mind of its own.

Three people, strangers to each other
in the outside world, all gathered
in a ten-foot by ten-foot room,
each taking a few moments to acknowledge
each other's presence, trying to find
and give the smallest bit of comfort
to a person they might not even speak to
if the circumstances were different.

Bill sits in his chair, praying and hoping
his wife will come out of this coma.
Lucy prays her daughter will be able to walk again
after her head-on-collision car accident.
And John is hoping and praying his first child
will simply be a healthy baby boy.

Sometimes we feel as if we are on top of the world.
As if we actually can control it.
Sometimes we are tossed about
Like so much sand in the wind,
And sometimes we are smashed like a tiny bug.
Sometimes we would do almost anything
to change the way things are.
Sometimes we would gladly put ourselves
in someone else's shoes.
Sometimes we pretend to have what we perceive
as control of safety.

But none of these prepares us for the time
we inevitably spend, gathered in a very small room
facing hours, days, and in the worst cases,
months and years,
finding out one of life's toughest lessons.

Sometimes we live our lives,
fill each moment with purpose or fantasy,
and sometimes, we can do nothing more
than simply pray and wait.

Ed Roberts 3/27/07
(Edited by Ursula Gibson)

In the past few years I have spent way too much
time in hospital waiting rooms and nursing homes.
I have watched so many people thumbing though
magazines and flipping channels on the television,
trying to find something that will comfort them.
This poem may become the title piece for another
Poetry For Life book to help those who find
themselves in these places.

In the End

I am the dreaded monster
The beast many fear
They deny me
Live to spite me
I fill their nightmares
Haunt them
From the very shadows
Of their simple existence

I am the gentle repost
The deliverer
From pain
From remorse
Many seek me
In ways only they can imagine
Beg for my calling
With each and every breath

Monster
Angel
Curse
Or blessing
In the end
I am but who I am

Death

Ed Roberts 2/21/07

In Search of Happiness

What is it that you want?
Have you ever stopped to think?
Is there one thing in the whole wide world
That would truly make you happy,
Make your life complete?

A new job perhaps?
Maybe a new car?
What about that really nice house
The one that sits on top of the hill?
Is this what it would take
For all your wishes to be fulfilled?

There is always money you know.
The only problem there though
Is how much?
How much is really enough?
Is there even such a thing?
Maybe it's something smaller,
Like a necklace or a ring?

What is it that you want?

I sit here alone
As I often do
Asking myself this question
And sharing these words with you.

For me the answer is simple.
I've tried to give it to you in rhyme.
For me
The one thing that I need to be happy
Is simply a little more time.

A simple phone call from my children
Or another picture of my grandchildren
To hang on the wall.
Maybe a lunch date with my sister
Or even a short e-mail from them all.

Another day
To play cards with my father,
Another evening to spend with my wife,
Another kiss on the cheek from my mother,
What more can a man ask for
To bring happiness into his life?

In the background
I hear the clock ticking.
Each one marks a second past.
And I smile through all these teardrops
For I know in the end
In life
It will be these special moments
That last.

Deep down I know
I will be happy
Even after I am gone.

Ed Roberts 1/06/06

Around the Peachtree

The roar of the planes
Ripped the quiet night

Soon the sky was lit with the flashes
Ground to sky lightning
As the anti-aircraft guns once again blared

The war had come
Again

From her gentle slumber
Misha was cruelly torn
Her mother's voice rang
Above the shrills of the falling bombs
The ground shook under her feet
As she leapt from her bed

She grabbed her rag doll Gwenna
Threw the blanket from her bed
Over her head
And like she had done so many times before
Followed her mother and sister out the door

Drenched with the rain
Surrounded by the chaos
Of exploding bombshells and cannon fire
They stood hand in hand
Under the lone peach tree
In front of her house

As quickly as it had started
The war left
New craters had been dug in the field

One of the small barns by the house had simply
disappeared
But once again
They had been spared
Left unharmed by the storm

Her mother had always told her
Bombs can't hurt us my dear
Not as long as we are standing
Hand in hand
Under this peach tree

In a world
Where no place was truly safe
Somehow those few words
Brought comfort and hope
To a child that knew no other world

The war like so many passed
Winners were declared
Losers and innocent alike suffered
And time moved on

In a field at the edge of what is now a bustling city
An old peach tree still stands
A constant reminder to us all
That even in a world
Not full of bombshells and gunfire
With a few simple words
Coined from a mother's love
We all can still find
A safe place to hide

Ed Roberts 12/20/06

Rosa hated the Soldiers

Rosa hated the soldiers
To her
It mattered not
Which uniform they wore

It wasn't her fault
That she lived in the small house
The one that sat on top of the hill
The hill
That overlooked the town below

They all seemed to want it

First the Nazis came
They made her house their
Headquarters

They draped her walls with their flag
The one that bore the symbol
The symbol that so many people
Would learn to fear and hate

They ran wires across every wall
Wires across the floor
They used her family's dinner table
For a desk
The one her great grandfather had made
So many years ago

In her own home
They made her their slave
She cooked for them
Cleaned up after them

And lay awake so many nights
In fear of them
She feared them most
When they held their parties
They would sing
And dance
Dance to music they played
On her mother's piano
The one they ruined later
By drenching it in beer
And later
In bullets

Yes
Rosa hated the Nazis
She was so happy to see them go

But then the Russians came

She never understood
A single word they said
They never seemed to speak actually
They always yelled at her
As if mere volume
Would help get across their point to her

They burned what was left of her piano
For firewood
They took all the wires
Bundled them neatly in small bales
And shipped them far away
She was glad to see the wires leave
But the holes in the walls that the Russians left
As they took them still remained
What upset her most about the Russians
Was the fact that they killed her toilet

One day two soldiers
Were in her bathroom
One decided to wash his potato
The meal that he had been given
To last the day

To him
He saw a bowl filled with water
Its true purpose
Was merely a mystery
He had never seen such a bowl before

He let the potato soak for just a minute
One can imagine his dismay
As he witnessed what happened
When he pulled the string
That hung by its side

His buddy did the only thing
A good soldier could do in this situation
He grabbed his rifle
And shot the evil bowl
The one that stole his friend's potato
He had to make sure
It would never steal another meal
Away from a soldier again

Rosa was so glad
That the Russians didn't stay long

Then
Of course
Came the Americans
At first
The Americans seemed to like her
And her little house

They fixed the holes in the walls
With plaster
They even found her a new toilet
Though they were the ones
That seemed to use it all the time

Their stay in her house
Almost seemed bearable
Until they noticed the bomb
The one that was lodged in the rafters
Of her roof

She told them
That it had been there
For nearly a year now
It simply dropped from the sky
One night
Made a crashing sound
That seemed to disturb the Nazis the most

They covered it with a tarp the next morning
Argued amongst themselves
For hours
And left it there when they left

The Russians
Didn't even notice it
Of course

They were too occupied
With killing her bathroom fixtures
She guessed
But to the Americans
This bomb seemed so important
They seemed to feel it was something
That had to be dealt with right away

They drew plans on papers
Ones they draped across
Her great grandfather's table

They laid out strategies
Detailed operations
On how to deal with this problem

In the end
They hooked up her ox
To her ox cart
Tied ropes around the bomb
And carefully lowered it inside

Things would have been fine
Had not the other soldiers come
The ones that had been hiding for the past few
months
In the old school building

The rifle fire frightened the ox
Who still strapped to the oxcart
Decided to make a run for it
To the field across the road

Of course the bomb
The one that had rested so peacefully
For all this long time
Decided to go off
It created such a loud roar
The soldiers stopped fighting

They stood there
Guns and hand
And watched
As Rosa fell to her knees

Weeping
Each decided there had been enough
Enough war
Enough fighting
At this small house on the hill

They all left rather quietly
Leaving Rosa finally to herself

Yes
Rosa hated all the soldiers

The ones that ruined her piano
The ones that shot her toilet
And especially the ones
That blew up her ox

Ed Roberts 12/31/05

(Written for Shorty)

"Reflections"

The wind that blew
This dead leaf to the ground
Essentially breathed into it
New life .

This once dried-out, bitter, and fragile leaf
Is now so beautiful,
Not even the coldest of winters
Can pull it from the heavens.

It hung patiently
Knowing one day it must fall.
In its future though
It found contentment.

At the feet of the saddest person on this Earth.
Did it come to rest.

Only they could see
The beauty that was this leaf.
Only this simple leaf
Could turn their frown upside down.

Though fragile it was,
It's power was beyond comprehension.
For It was but one leaf
That fell alone
That saved this dying soul.

Sadly enough, in the fall only the leaves
Remaining on the trees are admired.
The most beautiful go unnoticed
For they lay upon the ground.

Ashley Jordan

Ashley is my niece whom I am VERY proud of

A Message to a Friend

What is it
What are you looking for
At the bottom of that bottle

Are you trying
To stop the pain
Trying to stop the tears
Or maybe
Simply
Trying to stop
Yourself

Does it work

Are you running away from something
Something that you did
Something you didn't do
Or worse
Something that was done to you
By another

Do you even remember
Anymore
What it was
You are running from

No
I'm not here to chide you
Judge you
Or
Condemn you
This is not my place

I have seen many things
That took me
To the very edge of that bottle
As well
My friend
I really do understand

I also see
What the bottle takes away though

It might stop the tears
It might stop the pain
Yes
But only for a short while

But
In the end
It will stop you
As well

And that
My friend
Is the greatest loss of all

We still need you
Here

Ed Roberts 3/25/06

Final Moments

There is a moment in one's life
Where all the plans have faltered
You've used your last ounce of strength
The walls around you have shattered
You are on your knees
With hope stretched to its most extreme existence
The last drop of air has left your lungs burning
And you sit
All alone
Waiting
Waiting for everything to simply end

Yes
There is a moment like this for all of us

In that moment
That minute space between heartbeats
We can find our true self

We will either succumb to fate
Close our eyes
And pray that there is a Heaven
Or we find the spark
Pull from a power
That is much greater than ourselves
And breathe

Yes
There is a moment like this
In each and every life
And in some like mine
There are more

Ed Roberts 12/05/07

Find Me

Find me
If you can
Standing alone
Here amongst all the clutter
One of six billion smiling faces
Just a person you might simply pass
As you walk by down the street

Find me
If you can
I promise it will be worth your while
For you see
I want to be
Your friend

I will listen to your dreams
Share with you
Your hopes
I will really mean it
When I ask
How are you doing
When we meet each other on the street

So
Find me
If you can
It may take time
It might take a little effort
But as hard as you try
I promise
I will be trying just as hard
To find you

Ed Roberts 5/1/07

93

Angel Fallen

There was a time
Once
That I stood in the Heavens
Looked down on the humans
Saw the many evil things that they did
For the innocent I cried
Upon the unholy
I cried out for revenge

One day
My prayers were answered

Into one hand
Was placed the sword of justice
Into the other
The shield of virtue

Down into your world
I was sent
The deliverer of justice
To become

I was to be
Judge
Jury
And yes
Executioner
For all men to face

But
In those that I was sent to punish
I saw something
Something unexpected

Behind dead eyes
I saw a glimmer of hope
In the darkest of souls
I saw the ability to change
And in the most evil of hearts
Remained the remnants of
LOVE

From my own shoulders
I tore my silver wings
Deep into your highest mountain
I thrust my only sword

For in you
You humans
I saw the one thing
That I could not bring myself to destroy
Hope

I walk among you now
An angel fallen
Praying each night
That I have not made some grave mistake
Spending each waking hour
Trying to awaken in you
My now brothers
The true virtue
That each of you carry in your hearts

My destiny
To me
Remains unknown

Sometimes I feel my wings
Trying to thrust themselves from my spine
In the darkest of nights my sword calls to me
To once again let it rise
To punish the wicked

Through this treacherous journey
What you call life
I am left with but a simple shield
And a prayer
That somehow
You can change

For now
At the end of my days
I too
The angel fallen
Will share your fate

Ed Roberts 8/27/06

I scream into the heavens

Why do you love me

Knowing all the things I have done

Knowing all the secrets my soul hides

Why do you even care

The answer falls from the sky

Written on just a single snowflake

Because

Ed Roberts 2/16/07

Life

At the end

There is more

Ed Roberts 2/16/07

Perfection?

I'm not perfect
I'm too fat
I'm too short
My hair is turning white
What is not falling out that is
I also don't have any teeth any more
Lost those to the radiation a few years ago
Of course
I don't have any more tooth aches either
There can be a plus side to it you know
I also belch, scratch, and yes even fart way too often
But I guess you really didn't need me to say that
Did you

No
I'm not perfect
A hunk
I am not

I'm not perfect
I cry

I cry at a sad country song
A powerful poem
Yes, during a VERY good movie
I cry when I see tears
In my wife's eyes
In my children's eyes
My mother's eyes
Basically, yes
I cry when others cry

No
You can beat me in the back with a hammer
And not a single tear will I shed
But let my grandson hit his head on a table
It's crying time again

No
I'm not perfect
Like it or not
These eyes leak

I'm not perfect
My wife swears I snore
Of course she does as well
But getting either one of us to stop after 31 years
I know that's not going to happen
No, I'm not perfect
I snore

I'm not perfect
I dream

I dream when I sleep
I sometimes dream when I am awake
Though getting any of these to ever become reality
I know I'm not very good at that at all
Sometimes they do come close
Sometimes they might even become the dream of
another
But in this area
I know
I'm not perfect
But at least I try
And I still can dream

Well
There you have it
Plain and simple
Just like this man that stands before you

No
I'm not perfect

I'm just me

Ed Roberts 9/20/07

Heartbreak

Your lungs desperately gasp for air
That they simply can not find

You suddenly lose touch with your feet
And pray they will keep you
Held fast to the ground underneath

Your hands tightly grasp
Anything they might reach

The quivering starts
From your toes
To your lips
And quickly envelopes your entire being

The pressure behind your eyes builds
Stretching your eyelids
Until finally they can hold no more

In a moment of complete surrender
It happens

You release that first single tear

Yes
This is what happens
When a heart breaks

Ed Roberts 3/11/06

The Sentry

In the middle of the night
He awakens
The hail of bullets
Still ringing in his ears

Once again
He witnessed
The slaughter of innocence
Was forced to stand
Amongst the dying
And the dead

They were
So many nameless faces
Women
Children
Men he had never known
All victims of blind rage
And hate

Some were far too close
He called them "Friend"
"Buddy"
They were just like him
Taken from their world
Having given up their day-to-day
To be there by his side
But they would never make it home
For them
His heart bled the most

Yes
In the middle of the night

He awakens
Rescued once again
From the IED's
Whisked by the hands of time
Back into his here and now
A place that so many
Simply refer to as safe

Silently
He slips from the covers
Careful not to wake her again
From her much deserved slumber

In the darkness
He wipes the tears
The ones
No one would ever suspect
Eyes like his could shed

Quietly he drifts down the hallway
Into the small bedroom
On the left

At the foot of the bed
He takes his position
Sitting
Ever so still
On the floor
In the darkness
And listens to his son sleep

He has seen what the world had to offer
Bears his scars
Both inside and out
In silence
And understands far too well

The dangers that tomorrow can bring
So every night
One silent sentry takes his post
In a small bedroom
At the foot of a small bed in the corner
Sworn simply to protect
His and her future
Guarding their only son
From the evils
That we all call
Today

Ed Roberts 7/09/06

(For Chase)

Trial of Words

There is no pretense
No room for ego here
No lies
No mystery
No attempt to elude
No attempt to deceive
Here it is basic
Here it is simple

Here there is just a simple man
And his pen
Nothing more
Nothing less

Here I leave my heart
My dreams
My nightmares
All left on plain white paper
For you to see

Judge now for yourself
Whether these words
Are worth your time
And the tears I have shed
To lay them before you

Maybe
In the end
All I can give you is merely poetry
And if that is truly to be the case
Maybe that in itself
Will be enough

Ed Roberts 10/07/06

Askin' for It

You're askin' for it
She said
With a concerned look upon her face

I stopped what I was doing
And looked up at her

You're askin' for it
She repeated
And without giving me a chance to reply
She continued

Don't you worry about their threats
Do they have to kill you
To get your attention
Is that what you want

I stood up
Took my mother in my arms
And held her for just a moment

Yes, Mom,
I answered softly
I am askin' for it
In fact I am beggin' for it
And pleadin' for it
Each and every day

What you have to ask yourself, though,
Is what is it that I am askin' for

She backed up a bit
And looked into my eyes

It hasn't changed, Mom
I continued
From the very first day
I have asked for
And prayed for
But one thing

I want to be given the chance
The strength
And the faith
To change the world
Nothing more
Nothing less

What frightens me most
More than any threat they might deliver
Is that in a small way
I may have been given
Just a little bit
Of what I have been asking for

Yes, Mom
I am askin' for it
Today and tomorrow
And will continue to do so
As long as God allows

Ed Roberts 2/01/06

"Ask, and it shall be given"

Tears of a Soldier

A mother stops for a moment
At her mailbox
The flag is down
The mailman has come
And gone
It's been three months
Since her last letter from her son
The son who is now so far away
She whispers a prayer
As she reaches for the door of the box
And slowly reaches inside
"Nothing but bills"
She says out loud to herself
With a tone of relief in her voice
She quietly takes the hand full of envelopes
Into the house
Sits at the table and starts to open them
Still it has been three months
She sets aside the envelope in her hand
Bows her head
And whispers her prayer
"Please God
Keep him safe
Just one more day"
She reaches for a box of tissue
The one she keeps on the table
Just for this purpose
And gently wipes away her tears
Tears she cries for her son
The soldier

The telephone rings
It's nine PM
She rushes to try and catch it
Before the next ring
The baby has just fallen asleep
She pauses though
As she reaches for the receiver
It's been three months
Three long months since she has heard from her
husband
With hesitation in her voice she answers
"Hello"
She breathes a sigh of relief
It's his mother again
No mail today
They talk for nearly an hour
Try and convince each other
Everything will be "just fine"
She hangs up the phone and collapses on the sofa
Drowns the cushion once again with her tears
Tears she cries for her husband
Her husband that is 'working" so far away
Her husband the soldier

He crouches alone in an alley
"Safe" for the moment
From the hell that has constantly engulfed his world
It's been three months
He tells himself
They are probably worried sick
He pulls out his notepad and pen
And with the light of a broken streetlamp
He takes time to scribble just a few words

"Everything here is fine.
Miss yall more and more each day.
Take care of Nathan and most of all
Take care of each other."
He shoves the letter in a battered envelope
One of several
He keeps folded in his jacket
He plans to drop off
Whenever he gets the chance
If ever he gets the chance
He carefully stores his pen and paper
And once again gets back to work
Working at a job
He knows could at any moment end his life
Still someone has to be there
And he has seen what could happen
If no one was
As he slips back on his helmet
He wipes away the tears with his sleeve
Tears he tries so hard to disguise
For some might see them as a sign of weakness
Tears he cries
Far more often than he would like to admit
The tears of a soldier

Ed Roberts 11/08/06

The Colors of Our Nation

Red
The color of blood
A constant reminder to us that freedom is never free

White
The color of purity
Something we all should reach for in ourselves
Something we should strive to bring to others as well

Blue
The color of courage
A willingness to fight
And yes die
To protect the helpless
The weak
The poor
Our home
Our children
And our country

The flag
A simple piece of cloth
Transformed by these colors
Into a symbol
One we all should cherish
Respect and treasure
For within its stars and stripes
Lies both our past and our future

As long as it waves
Freedom
Is more than simply a dream

Ed Roberts 10/17/06

Us vs. Them

I met a man from Jordan yesterday
We talked of my trip there
I told him of my poem
Flowers for the Tank
Of how I would move the tank away
Away from our embassy there
And plant flowers in its place

He looked at me and smiled
No, sir
You would not want to do this
He said
The terrorists would attack you
Kill you if they could

I looked at him
For just a moment
Waited for his next breath
And asked

Who are the terrorists
The ones that I must fear

He stopped
I could see his thoughts
As they pressed upon his heart

He dropped his head
Set his eyes upon the floor
And in the softest of voices
Spoke

The terrorists are us

I reached out
Gave him my hand
And replied

No, my friend
You or I could never be one of them
And if more people stopped to ask this question
More will realize
They are one of us instead

When there are enough of us
There will never be
Any more of them
Again

Ed Roberts 2/18/06

Child Forgotten

Who are you
Man-child
I thought I knew you once

You walked barefoot
Through my forest
Swam in my rivers and lakes
I fed you
Clothed you with skins from my children

During the day
Bathed you with my sunlight
At night
Covered your head with stars

Who are you
Man-child
Who are you now

You covered my meadows
With concrete
Poured your filth Into my rivers and lakes
Choked the birds from the sky
With your soot

You chop
You dig
You burn
You dredge
You take everything
You give nothing back

What am I to do
My Man-child
There is only so much water
No more
No less

I have only so much land
If you take it all
There is nothing left

What of your brothers
The elk
The wolf
The hawk
And the buffalo

What would you have me tell them
This is their world as well

Who are you now
My man-child

Are you my keeper
Are you my destroyer
Are you my child
Or my reaper

Understand this
My man-child

In the end
Our fates are both
Just one

Ed Roberts 1/24/07

Shoes

When we are born
We each are given
A single pair of shoes
To travel upon this path
That we call "Life"

Like any pair of shoes
They can get scuffed
Worn down around the edges
And sometimes
They really do not seem to fit at all

We take them with us always
Sometimes down paths we shouldn't
Sometimes where others would not dare tread
We wear them through storm and sun the same

Some give them little regard
Some pamper and polish them
Trying their best to extend their use
Far beyond their intended lifespan

Occasionally a person can trip or fall
Lose one or both for no apparent reason
Only then does one realize
There truly is one pair per customer
Once lost here
They can not be replaced

One thing in life is certain
At the end of our journey
At the edge of our path
All shoes finally do wear out

Alongside the edge of this walkway
Awaits for us a chair
One in which we all finally must sit
To rest

This my friend
Is where faith is born

When we get to this chair
In our final moment
We will either find waiting for us
Nothing at all
Or if we have left behind us
Enough hope and love
Beside this single chair
Awaits for us
A new pair of shoes

Ed Roberts 12/26/06

Death of a Child hood

We were young back then
Dennis and I
Growing up way too fast
Or trying to

He and I were very close
He was closer to me
Than my brother
But that in itself is a different poem

I was the straight kid
The geek
The one that didn't seem to fit in with most
He was somewhere on the other side
He lived alone with his mother
Didn't really care much for school
He had no relationship with his father
It would always make him happy
When I let him borrow mine

We were just two kids
Growing up in different worlds
That fate put together
Both were the better for it
Though some would argue about this

Dennis went the way of alcohol
And yes
Even messed around with pills as well
He kept a gun in a shoebox
One he kept hidden in his room
Then later he hid it under the seat of his car

I often wonder
What my other friends would have thought
If they knew I had one hidden too
Not everything was as peaceful as it seemed
Some serious trouble would sometimes come my
way
But there again that is a different poem as well

I remember the last day I talked with Dennis
He was leaving school to marry his girlfriend
She was expecting their child
Both of them were seventeen

We were standing in the hallway at school
I saw he was carrying his pistol in his coat
Later that night
The phone rang
They said that Dennis and another friend had been
drinking
Something had gone wrong
Somehow the gun went off
And the bullet went through the side of Dennis's
head

No one would listen
When I told them that for the gun to go off
Someone would have to pull the trigger twice
The chamber under the hammer was always empty
Along with the first one as well
He learned this from me

One never knows
When they might be facing their own gun
This gives you a second
That the other person doesn't know about
Sometimes every second counts

The next few days are still a blur
I kept on working
I kept on living my normal life
Except when I wasn't at work or at home
I was hunting
Hunting for the man that killed my friend
The one that took him from this world

Luckily the police found him first
I say that even though they later let him go
Still
Had I found him
My life would be very different than it is today

I helped carry Dennis's casket at his funeral
We buried his mother that day as well
Even though it took years for her to join him
Her soul went with his that day
I remember the last day I saw her
She handed me the keys to his car
She asked about Maria
But neither of us ever heard from her again

That night
After every one else had gone to bed
A young boy took a small box out of his closet
And left his house without making a sound

He went to a small field not far away
Dug a small hole with his father's shovel
And in it
Buried the box

In this box
There was a pack of Marlboros
Smoking would never be cool to him again

There was a small bottle of pills
Pills he had taken from his brother
Pills that he took sometimes
When he couldn't take the pain
A picture of his best friend
One he would carry with him
In his heart for the rest of his life
And pieces of a broken gun
One he had smashed the day before
When no one else was home

Yes
There were several burials that day
Earlier I was there
When they put my best friend's body into the ground
I saw the death of a woman's soul
As she turned to drive away in her car
And later that night
I went alone into an empty field
And buried part of my soul and my childhood
In a small box

Childhood is a time for learning
Often lessons are learned
That come with a very high price

Ed Roberts 1/13/06

*I got married and became a father at the age of
eighteen. My sons often wondered why it was so
important to me that I knew what was in their closet,
in their dresser drawers, and under their bed.
Both are grown now, my oldest is a father as well
Now they both understand if they didn't before.*

The Scent of Death

The scent of death
For all of those that have come across it
Reeks of an odor
One can never forget

It repels every cell in your body
Causes your stomach to churn and shrivel
Both at the same time
One can detect its presence
From many yards away
And its scent lingers on all it touches
No matter how hard we clean
Or try to disinfect
No
The scent of death
For so many reasons
Stays

I am left to wonder
What if lies were the same
What if they soured the tongue
Each and every time
As they passed on their way to our lips
What if they reeked of deceit
As they passed out the mouth
Left stains of ignorance
On all the ears they reached

Why must honor die in silence
It leaves without a single scent
No crackle when it is broken
It slips away with nothing
Leaving but an empty shell
With no stain left behind

Tasteless lies that kill honor
Honor that dies without a trace
Both of which
Most often lead to death

A scent
Far too many of us
Are very familiar with

Ed Roberts 5/15/07

Prayers to the Sun

Rugged hands grasp the wooden handle
The hoe chisels against unforgiving soil
Shallow furrows are carved
With so much blood, sweat, and tears
Precious depositories gained at such a high price
Shallow graves dug for priceless seed

With silver droplets
The farmer baptizes them
With water he has carried
From the last surviving stream
He raises his head to the heavens in prayer
Only to have the angry sun
Bake his face with its fury

The sun killed all the clouds
That dared shield the ground from its furious rage
Sixty days
And not a single gift of water
The farmer is merely left to wonder
Just how long can the Sun God's anger last

He covers each seed with care
Hoping to seal in each precious drop of moisture
And leaves his desert field
Holding only the slightest bit of hope
Through parched lips
Once again
He silently prays
For rain

Lightning flashes
The roar of thunder
Rolls across the tree tops
Shaking the wooden towers
To their very roots
The water returns in sheets
Pounding the saturated ground beneath

A farmer sits on his porch
Slowly rocks back and forth
Another five acres were lost last night
Taken away by what used to be his fishing pond
The river broke its banks on Friday
Now it is threatening the road
He wonders how long he has
Before it comes for the house as well

The spring wheat washed away in early February
He jokes to himself
Maybe he should have planted rice instead
Deep inside though he knows time isn't on his side
Crops can't grow until they are planted
And right now
His tractor is wheel-deep in mud

He rises slowly from his rocker
Inside he starts another pot of coffee
And in a gentle voice
He prays
He prays for the Sun
To once again
Return

Two men
Worlds apart
Different in so many ways
Each offering words of prayer
To an unforgiving god
That has long since
Forgotten their names
As they forgot
His

Ed Roberts 5/11/07

Miracles

After you have
Explored every possibility
Weighed every option
Tested and re-tested every theory
Ruled out the plausible
Explained away all the maybe's
The could be's
And even all the should be's
When you examined
And reexamined all the facts
And still you are left with no real explanation
Then and only then
Are you truly able to accept
That miracles do happen
And yes
Sometimes they can even happen
To you

Ed Roberts 3/22/05

The Finish Line

A mile in another man's shoes is still a mile
The distance is shorter for no one
The strength of the legs matters not
For it is the strength of the heart that feeds them
That determines who will reach the finish
And who will be left behind

Ed Roberts 11/01/07

Of the People

A government is made up of people
It is created to protect and serve their needs

People need freedom

Freedom
To work
To pray
To love
To live
To raise their family
To speak
To be heard
Freedom to be
Themselves

A government should be
Of the people
For the people
And
By the people

It should exist solely for their benefit

People make laws
Laws protect their property
Their lives
And their freedom
Laws are enforced by their government

In this world
People should never live in fear
Of their laws
Of their freedom
And most of all
Of their government

A government that fails to realize this
Must always live in fear of the people
For whom it was once created
To serve

Ed Roberts 5/30/07

Rivers to the Sea

Hate
Breeds more hate

Guns
Bring more guns

Blood
Brings more bloodshed

Death
Brings more death

All of these
Are rivers
That run strong and deep

All empty
Into the sea
Of chaos and despair

Along each river
At the foot of every sea
There lies a shore

Only upon this soil
Can we ever find peace

Trust
Hope
And love
Are the winds
That will guide us there

Faith
Is the only anchor
Strong enough
To prevent our return

Ed Roberts 2/13/06

Homeland Security

I will protect you
From your enemy

I will watch over you
To keep you safe

I will screen your mail
So that they can not poison you

I will watch your home
So they can not break in

I will follow you to work
So they can not harm you
Or take you along the way

I will follow your children to school
So that they can not take them
As well

I will watch you at work
To keep you and your employees safe

I will read your e-mail
Both at work and at home
So they can not attack you with a virus

I will be at the grocery store
So that they can not poison your food

I might suggest what you buy there
So that you do not poison yourself

I will read your newspapers
So that they will not expose you
To their threats and ideas

I will watch your television
So I can protect you there the same way

I will monitor your bank account
So that they can not steal from you

I will follow you to church
To protect your freedom to worship

I will even watch your minister
To make sure he does not become one of them

I will even listen to your prayers at night
To protect your right to pray

I will make your life safe
I will make your life secure
I will protect you from your enemies
And let you know who they are

I will make sure
That you have all that you need

I will try and make sure
That you have all that you want

I can give you almost everything
Of course
None of this will be cheap

I will need to take some of your money
To pay for all of these things

But isn't security like this
Worth a small price
You'll hardly notice
What it is I take away
I'll only remove it
A small piece at a time

Remember
It is for your own good
And the good of everyone else

Freedom has its price
But so does security

In the end
It is up to you to decide
Which you value most

Ed Roberts 3/27/06

BEG

For another glass
Is what you ask
To wash away your pain
Just one more to wash your tears
But nothin's left except the stain

I've got another bottle on the shelf
Just in case you ever find yourself

You leave your troubles at the door
Every time that you walk in
But you leave here want'n more
It's just a road that never ends

How much did it cost
To lose your life this way
Your soul is what you've lost
And you haven't got a dime to pay

For another glass
Is what you plead
As I throw you out the door
In the gutter
On your knees you cry
And beg for more

How much did it cost
To lose your life this way
Your soul is what you've lost
And you haven't got a dime to pay

So beg

Ed Roberts 2/11/06

Memorial

They gather in silence
Rows of men and women
Some in wheelchairs
Others with their walkers
Old and young
Standing shoulder to shoulder
Some broken
By time
And circumstance
Each with their own story to tell

Donald served with Patton
Drove his jeep
Across most of Europe

Jessie was at Pearl Harbor
Watched the first planes fly over
Lost his leg later that day

Michael served in Korea
Was shot five times
Before they finally sent him home
He said that he'd go back tomorrow
But at 72
I doubt there is much of a chance

Mary went to Vietnam
As a nurse
Was shot in the hip by a sniper
She stayed for hours with the injured
Before she finally got help for herself

Bill was injured in Desert Storm
The first one
At 34
He stands out amongst his elders
A reminder to us all
War does not discriminate
When it comes to its victims
He too would serve tomorrow
If he only had his legs

Before these heroes
Young men in uniform present the colors
We all share a pledge
Whose words were paid for
By these and so many others

Seven men march to the center of a field
Raise their rifles
And fire to the heavens
Three times each
Twenty-one shells in all
Fall to the grass at their feet

Names are read of the fallen
A bell tolls for each one
The list goes on as everyone listens
A father or brother
Some just another man's friend
A special name
They each hope to hear

After the last name is read
Taps echoes across the pavilion

Men who stood in the face of horror
Try to wipe away their tears
Before others notice

With a short prayer
The ceremony is over
Just another Monday for so many
A day to kick off their summer

For me
A Memorial Day
I will always remember
For on this day
I rang the bell for my Father
And this simple chime
Rings in me still

I walk away slowly
With an empty shell casing in my pocket
Held closely
To my heart

Ed Roberts 5/29/06

Each Step

Each step takes me farther down the path
Surrounded by nothing but water
I travel in thirst
Questions like waves crash into my soul
All leading to that precious moment
When I finally reach the end
When I take that last step
Will I truly be able to walk on water
And leave this world behind
Or will I sink and drown forever
In regret
Each step takes me farther down the path
The only thing that is certain
Is that it's far too late to go back now

Ed Roberts 6/05/07

Stone in the Hand

Taken from the very heart of the Earth
Hardened by the fires of Her passion
Weathered by so many storms
Strong to its very core
I am the rock
Yet gently in your palm I rest
Listening to the whispers of your soul
Sharing with you the secrets of mine
I am the rock
I am you
We are one

Ed Roberts 7/16/07

The Pledge

It was seventh grade
I remember my first day of school
The day started out the normal way
We all went into the classroom
Found our seats
A new teacher stood before us
His name written on the board

The morning announcements started
None of us paid much attention
When it came time
We were all asked to stand
For the "Pledge of Allegiance"
Most of us stood
Not all
Some remained seated
Too busy talking to their friends
Too busy even to notice
How this affected the man that stood in front of the
class

When the announcements finished
Senor Cortez silently walked over and closed the
doors to the room
He took the book he was holding in his hands
Probably the attendance book
And slammed it against the chalkboard
This
Of course, got our attention

He stood before us
Tears trickling down his face
And began to speak

When I was a child
I grew up in Cuba
There was a day much like today
I remember going to school
I was only seven or eight though
Soldiers came to my school that day
Several men in uniforms I had never seen before
Three of them walked into my classroom
Two started beating my teacher
The third stood at the front of the room
And held a gun pointing in our direction
The men dragged our teacher from the classroom
We all sat there
Terrified to move

We sat there for what seemed like hours

Another soldier came into the classroom
Spoke to the first
And we were all led out of the school
Single file
Into the courtyard

Our teacher was there
Broken
Beaten
On her knees in front of a soldier

One of them spoke to us
He told us
Things were never going to be the same again
With this the one soldier lowered his rifle
And shot our teacher
Right in front of us

Another soldier took an American flag
He had found in the school
Stomped on it
Poured gasoline on it
And set it afire with his cigar
Into this fire they threw our books
We were sent home after that
That was the last day
I was ever allowed to go to my school
They burned it that afternoon

Children
And you are still children to me
There is a lesson here
That I want you to never forget

Every time you are asked to stand here in my
classroom
To take a few moments of your morning
To pledge allegiance to this wonderful flag before
you
I want to remember that you are doing so
Along with a man
That does remember what it means
To have all of this wonderful freedom you enjoy
Taken away

If you are to say "The Pledge of Allegiance" here in
this classroom
You will do so
With all the respect and dignity
That these words deserve
If you can not do this children
I will make you leave

From that day forward
Even into today
These special words
The ones we call "The Pledge of Allegiance"
Hold a special place in my heart
For I remember a special lesson
That a very special man took the time to teach us
Not simply about Cuba
But about life as well

Ed Roberts 10/17/06

Lessons

Life
It's not about what you have behind you
What you did
Last week
Last month
Last year

No
These are merely footprints
That determine
Where you are now
Upon the path

Life
It's not about
The damage you left behind
The bridges you burned
The mistakes you've made
The baggage you now carry

Bridges can be rebuilt
Everyone makes mistakes
You can decide to leave baggage behind
At any time

Life is about choices
Not so much
The choices you have made
But your next choice
And the next

Life is a path
Determined by simple

And not so simple steps
Each one in its own way
Priceless
Each one a journey
In and of itself

If you find yourself
Going the wrong way
You can always stop
And change direction

If there is no path
Where you need to go
You can always be the first
Who knows
Maybe others will follow

Every life
Can have meaning
Every life
Can have purpose
Every life is precious
Yes,
Even yours

Life is forgiving
The more you forgive
The more you are forgiven

Life is about love
The more you love
The more you are loved
By others

Life is the teacher
Life is the lesson
In the end
Life is the final exam

The best any of us can hope for
In the end
Is to receive a passing grade
Otherwise we might have to repeat the class
Over and over again
Until we finally get it right

Ed Roberts 7/16/07

Life House

To build a house
Someone must shape the bricks
Someone must cut the timbers
Someone must lay a foundation
Someone must shore the walls
Someone must lay a floor
Someone must frame a roof
Someone must install the plumbing
Someone else must provide for power
Someone must install the windows
And
Someone must hang the doors

Each of these in its own way
Reeks of its own insignificance

In the end
However
Miss the efforts of one single person
And the entire house
Fails to fulfill its purpose

Is this not the same
In building one's life
As well

Ed Roberts 6/20/06

Remembrance

When I was younger
To some 30 isn't very young though
I had the opportunity to spend a few months
At least part of a few months
In Chicago

I was learning what I could still do
My legs were healing from being burned
Each day I could walk farther and farther
And my Grandfather was always there
There with words of encouragement when I needed
them
There with a shoulder and a backhand
When I needed those as well
My life had gone through changes
He was there
To keep those changes going in the right direction

I remember we would often stop
At a little Chinese restaurant
Between our many errands that we seemed to be
constantly running
It really wasn't much of a restaurant though
Probably fifteen to twenty tables
But the food there was simply delicious
And it sat right in the middle of what is known as
Chicago's Chinatown

You could sit at your table
Talk about almost anything
Or simply listen to all the wonderful sounds
That seemed to seep in from all around you
Take you places in your mind

You have never been before
On a street corner
Just outside this little restaurant
There sat an old man
Everyday we stopped by
He would be sitting there on his homemade blanket
Playing a two-stringed instrument softly
Gently with his bow
The sounds that came from this corner were
amazing

I would stop sometimes
Stand there as the different cars and buses drove by
And listen with my Grandfather
As this man seemed to literally
Make his simple Morin Khur speak

At first the old man seemed oblivious of our
presence
But after we had stood there a few times
And of course laid a few dollars on the blanket at his
feet
He would smile each time he saw us
And somehow
Though one would never think it possible
Play his simple instrument a little better than before

This went on for a few weeks
Every time our path took us anywhere near this little
place
Near being ten miles in Chicago's standard
We would stop and eat at this Chinese restaurant
And listen to our own private recital
That of course we would share
With anyone else that was walking by

I was coming towards the end of my stay there
My legs were getting better
The fair season was coming to a close
(This is what my Grandfather did for a living
Sewed names on hats
And sold different items at State Fairs)
We stopped by what had become
Our favorite meeting place
To grab a bite and rest from the daily hustle
That only Chicago can seem to muster

We had not been there long
When we realized something was missing
The food was still delicious
The buses and cars still drove past
But gone was our recital
No music filled the air

We walked over to the street corner
The mat still remained at its spot
Beside it stood a wooden cart
From which a young man was selling hotdogs
Or a Chinese version thereof
In Chicago this somehow didn't seem odd at all

On top of the mat sat his Morin Khur
The bow rested by its side
Next to these was a simple note
Temujin played here

We stood there for a moment side by side
Closed our eyes and listened
You could somehow still hear this gentle instrument
speak

We both placed a twenty on the blanket
The young man behind the cart gave us a gentle
Thank you
And we went about our way

In that single moment
Each of us had shared a blessing
And given an old man
One who had given so much to people he never
knew
The one thing he deserved the most

Remembrance

In the end
None of us can ask for more

Ed Roberts 1/09/07

Headlines

It is pasted there in the headlines

**Rival Kenyan Tribes Face Off With Machetes, Clubs
and Rocks in Once Quiet Tourist Town
Militia kill 21 in West Darfur
Gunmen in Guyana kill 5 kids, 6 adults
Congo massacre leaves 1,000 dead
Scores die in Sri Lanka clashes**

*To so many
These are simply stories
Something that happens to "those' people
Over there*

*To so many
This is too far away to really care about
No
Nothing like this could ever happen here*

We have our own headlines to worry about

**Studios strike deal with writers
US network faces $1m nudity fine
First-grader gets suspension for loaded gun
Jury Selection to Begin in Ohio for Mother Accused
of Microwaving Month-Old Baby Case**

*Yes
These are closer to home
Still to most just so many words
Spread across the top of a paper
Nothing more*

No
We start our day
Reading the paper
Set it aside
And go about our "normal" life

We go to work
Do our job
And at the end of the day
Go back home

We enjoy our homes
Our families
Our things

On the weekends
We watch TV
Go to a movie
Maybe go out of town
To see someplace
We have never seen before

To us
These headlines
Are words with no meaning
Posted across a paper
That at the end of the day
We can toss away with the trash
And silently sometimes at night
We pray
That this is all they will ever be
To us

There are some things in this world
No amount of words can change

There are some things
That can not be changed with
Love
Understanding
Hope
Laws
Education
Legislation
Or
Even money

No
These things can make this world a better place
These are things we all are in desperate need of
But still there are some things in this world
That will remain unchanged
Even with all of these

There are some things in this world
That can only be changed
With blood

Still
After all this blood
After all these headlines

Why is it
Things still never seem
To change

Ed Roberts 1/28/08

Three Grains of Sand

In my hand
I hold three grains of sand.

Examine each one carefully,
Closely.

Which of these
Is worth taking the life of an innocent
To possess?

Which of these
Is worth giving your own life
To obtain?

Which is worth
The lives of your children
And their children
To secure?

I lay at your feet
Nothing but three single grains of sand.
They lay there
Long before either of us was born.
They will lie there
Long after both of us are forgotten.

How much blood must we wash them in
Before we see them for what they truly are?
Nothing
But three simple pieces of Earth.

Ed Roberts 12/10/05

Rape

It's not about sex
It's not about lust
It's about power
And domination
It's all about
Control

You would make me your victim
Would you
Leave me shattered
Naked
Broken
Like you did all the rest
Ah, yes
That's what you had in mind
Didn't you

In this world
There are two roles
There is predator
And then there is prey

Mistake me for the latter
Did you
No
Not this time
Your instincts misled you
As I did

You do not have the power here
This time
The power and the control
Are all mine

You think I want you to stop
Do you
You think I am going to run away
Like a child
Screaming for help

Hmmm
No, I don't think so

Go ahead
I know what you had planned
We can still have sex
Who knows
Maybe I will enjoy it

You had better hope so

You see
I am the one in charge now
In the end
I will be the one who leaves here happy
This gun in my hand dictates that
You will satisfy me
One way or the other

Now
It's all up to you
Go ahead
Let's play

Ed Roberts 7/18/07

(Written for a friend who was a rape victim and
who is now a martial arts instructor.)

Murdered by the Mob

It was the pusher
That killed my son
If he hadn't sold him the drugs
My son would still be alive
It is his fault
The blame is on him
My hate
My anger
My loss
Is his to own

It was the supplier
That killed my son
If he hadn't brought the drugs here
In the first place
My son would still be alive
No
He never met my son
Never knew his name
But it is his fault
My son is dead
My hate
My anger
My loss
Is his to own

It was the grower
That killed my son
If he hadn't planted the poppies
My son would still be alive
I wonder if he knows
How many sons and daughters he has killed
Simply to survive

I wonder if he has a choice at all

No
He never met my son either
But it is his fault my son is dead
My hate
My anger
My loss
Is his to own as well

A not-so-innocent boy
My child
I buried in the ground today
He was slaughtered
By a mob of faceless murderers
People I hate
With every ounce of my being
And I am left here
Alone
To try and fill in the hole
That so many helped to dig

Ed Roberts 8/15/07

The hand that lifts the bottle

The glass is always empty
When it rests there on the shelf

The bottle always starts out full
One would not buy one if it wasn't

You always have a choice

You can drive right by
If you want
There are always much better places
For you to go

You stop
Out of anger
Out of grief
Out of habit
It doesn't matter why

No
You stop
Because somewhere deep inside
You want to

The bottle gets opened
The glass get filled
And you drink

It's not the bottle's fault
The glass always remains blameless
You can curse the hand that pours
If you wish

But if it wasn't theirs
It would simply be your own

The hand that lifts the bottle
Isn't the one that takes the glass to your lips
That hand my friend
Is yours

In the end
There is no one left to blame
But yourself

Ed Roberts 4/18/07

161

Have a Drink

You've had a hard day at the office
Here, have a drink

Your boss was on your ass today
You were late again
Here, have a drink

You lost your job today
Ten years down the tube
Here, have a drink

You've got bills building up on the table
No money left in the bank
Here, have a drink

You had another fight with your wife today
How the hell could she understand
Here, have a drink

You didn't go out to look for a job today
Decided to stay home instead
Here, have a drink

Another fight at home again
This time she said she was leaving
Taking the kids with her
Here, have a drink

You went and filed for assistance today
Good for you
Here, have a drink

You slept last night at the bus station
Saved a little change
So you might eat something today
Here, have a drink

Passed out and woke up at the hospital
Doctor said your liver is shot
Here, have a drink

Everything you loved is gone
Now you've only got a few more months to live
Here, have a drink

Why not
It's all you've got left

Ed Roberts 2/07/07

Alcoholism

It's there waiting
Always in the background
Just at the edge of sight and mind

Every time we reach out
It also reaches
Hoping simply for the slightest opportunity
To grab hold

We pretend to ourselves
It doesn't exist
Not for us
Somehow we are out of reach
We tell ourselves
We are the ones in control

These are the words
It lives for
These are the words
Off which the monster feeds

With each beer
Each glass of wine
Each after-dinner drink
We step into reach

No
Surely one can't hurt me
I can even handle two or three
Or is it
Four or five

Getting drunk once never killed anyone
Has it
I've been there before
I'm still here

No
One won't hurt

Still
It's there waiting
Always in the background
Just at the edge of sight and mind

Every time we reach out
It also reaches
Hoping simply for the slightest opportunity
To grab hold

I dance this dance myself
Knowing that the monster waits
Even for me

I tell myself
I can handle it
Just a glass of wine every now and then
And to myself
Silently I pray
I stay out of the monster's grasp

Ed Roberts 2/09/07

Judgment in the Dark

You asked for UNDERSTANDING
But gave none

You asked for TOLERANCE
But gave not an inch

You demanded RESPECT
But spat on the beliefs of others

You said you wanted PEACE
But in the air
You waved your gun

You wailed about your PERSECUTION
But slaughtered innocents
By the dozens

You killed by proxy
Maiming all that you could
Attacking from the shadows
Gloating in the daylight of fallen enemies
That you yourself refused to face

You beg me now for MERCY
As I bury the bodies of children
That you have left in your wake

Understanding
Tolerance
Respect
Peace
Mercy
None of these

You have shown
Persecution
You have yet to fully comprehend

It is beyond the reach of my soul
To punish you
To give you just reward for your actions
I can not do
And still live with myself afterward

Naked and bound
I shall render you
Alone in the dark
I shall toss you

Your last days
Hours
And moments
You shall spend preparing
To face the One
Capable of your judgement

Your memory in time
I shall erase
Ever to forget
As you become one of many
To see the darkness
And total isolation
Of the place I call
My Oubliette

In the end
I shall seal your remains
In mortar
So the Earth Herself
Will not have to absorb
Your vile soul

Ed Roberts 7/19/06

For the world to understand and finally achieve
Peace
It first must learn the meaning of Love
And rid itself
Of Prejudice and blind Hate

One Inch Closer to Heaven

I could reach down
And move the pebble resting at my feet
One inch
And I doubt
Anyone on Earth
Would be impressed much

Right now there are around
6.7 billion people
On this planet

If each of us in turn
Was to come along
And move this very same stone
Just one inch
When we were finished
This small rock
Would have traveled
105,745 miles

All I ask of you today
A very small request indeed
Is to go out into this small world of ours
And move it just one inch
In the direction of Heaven
Just one inch
That's all I ask
And tomorrow
And the day after that
Go out there
And do the same

Ed Roberts 12/21/07

Power

You have bullets
Guns to fire them
And soldiers to carry these

You have bombs to drop from planes
Missiles you can launch
From the sea, ground, or air

All of these you have
To use at your command
Against anyone you choose

You think somehow
That this gives you power

But you can make
Only so many bullets
There can only be a certain amount of guns
And you will have soldiers
Only as long as there are people
Who agree to become so

Your power is plastic
It melts in the heat
The heat that we generate
With mere words

Us
You can kill
But these words
They shall live forever

Freedom
Love
Faith
and Hope

Against these
You have no power at all

Ed Roberts 10/11/07

The War on Drugs

I am a drug dealer
Yes, the one you hate

I feed my family
What food I can afford
By moving boxes
Boxes filled with poison
Poison which you crave

My children have to eat

You sit in your fine homes
And curse my name to God
In your eyes
I am responsible

I kill your children
I breed your crack whores
All your drug problems
Your shootings
Your gang wars
Are my fault

You send soldiers
Men in uniform to burn my house
Men with guns
To kill my family

The cameras roll
Headline after headline
Is slapped across your papers
You measure the progress of your war
By the fatalities of my people

Still the boxes come and go
Still I fill them
Send them on their way

To you
I am a drug dealer
Yes, the one you hate
And as long as the money comes
I can truly live with that
And so will my children

In the end
I have no other choice

Ed Roberts 11/29/07

This is a dangerous topic.
One of my editors misunderstood this as somehow
promoting drug use. Yes, sometimes I step to the
edge with some of my writing I have talked to
several. people from Mexico including one of their
politicians. They told me that our desire for drugs is
killing their country. We as a government spend
huge amounts of money trying to destroy the
supply side of the drug problem. As long as there
are huge amounts of money to be made
providing the drugs people will find a way to make
them. Those in power care less for those that
their industry destroys. To stop the flow of drugs we
need to work harder on the demand side of the
problem.
If no one wanted them there would be no market for
them.

Death of Innocence

Do you remember
The first lie
That you ever told

Was it to someone
You loved
Cared for
Or maybe
Was it simply
To yourself

Do you remember
The first time
That you took something
That belonged to someone else

Was it something
Of importance
Of great value
Or was it something
You merely thought you wanted
Instead

Have you ever struck anyone
From rage
From anger
Or worse yet
From hate

Did they strike you back
Were they able to

Each of these
Are passing moments
Probably ones
We have long since forgotten
But inside we carry them
More than as mere memories
For by their passing
We witness
Another death of our own innocence

A death from which
We can buy no resurrection

Forgiveness becomes
Our very last hope

Ed Roberts 1/20/06

Five Minutes

Five minutes after your last breath

It will not matter
What car you drove
How much money you made
How big of a house you lived in

It will not matter
What position you held at your company
How many people worked for you
Or how many people were your superior

Meaningless will be
Your bank account
Your stock portfolio
The number of platinum cards
You possessed

Five minutes after your last breath
Irrelevant will be
The color of your eyes
The color of your hair
Even the color of your skin

Into this world
You came
Naked
Helpless
Void of all possessions

From this world
We all will leave
The same

Five minutes after your last breath
Your legacy is born

A litany of memories
Love you gave
Or lost
Love you destroyed in others

Tears you cried
Tears you caused
Memories carried by others
Or worst of all
Memories forever forgotten

Five minutes after your last breath
So many questions will be answered

Is there a God
Is there a Heaven
And most important to some
Is there really a Hell

Three hundred single seconds
Followed by an eternity
Of either
Never ending joy
Or regret

Five minutes
After your last breath

Ed Roberts 7/28/06

Self Portrait

Our life is but a painting
Each day
A different stroke

With every smile
We add a touch of vibrancy
Each tear
A hue of shade

We smear the edges
With anger
Shred the canvass with hate
Paint over our trespasses
In hope that somehow later
They find no way to bleed through

Hopefully
We add faces of loved ones
And friends that we hold dear
The names themselves
May in time escape our memory
But one never forgets
A smile or a loving touch

When our days here are over
We are left with nothing
But a simple painting
A self portrait
One whose paint has finally dried

We leave this world
With but one hope
A prayer if you will
That when we arrive
Back home to Heaven
God will be able to take one look
A glance at this single picture
We carry in our soul
And be able to recognize
Us
As one of His own

Ed Roberts 5/5/06

Prayer for a New Life

All the pages are waiting, empty
Comes now the opening chapter "Birth"
Followed by pages and pages of triumphs and
mistakes
Friends that came and went
A "First" love followed by real love
Followed by moments of joy and hours of heartache
Pages written so quickly
Stolen moments between family and work
And read over and over again
Once the days become shorter
And slip into silent memories
Withered hands finally place it upon the shelf
And with last breath a dream is whispered
A silent prayer for there to be a new book waiting
With new pages for a new life

Ed Roberts 2/5/07

Genius

I knew a genius once
He sewed names on hats for people
At State fairs
He drove an old Chevy station wagon
That had almost 500,000 miles on it
He never wore a suit
Shaved sometimes
And his language at times
Could make a sailor blush
I didn't get to spend much time with him
But I truly feel like we came to know
And understand each other
Yes, I knew a genius once
His name was Henry
He was my Grandfather

I knew another genius
He worked for a railroad company
Before he hurt his back
He traveled down many wrong roads
But in the end
Spent a lot of his time
Trying to help others find the right one
His name was David
He was my uncle
Henry's son
Like Henry
I didn't get to spend a lot of time with him
But he and I did get to know
And understand each other
But like Henry
David is now gone

I know another genius
No
He's not a doctor, lawyer, scientist
Or even a teacher
He's worked in restaurants
A machine shop
And now
Makes car reservations for people
He really is just any ordinary man
Like me

I am Henry's grandson
I am David's nephew
And yes
I am a genius as well

It doesn't make me special
It doesn't make me smarter than you
In so many ways
It doesn't help much at all
But I am what I am
Like it or not
This is something I can not change

Imagine having a thought
So pure
So clear
It's like seeing the perfect rose
Or a brilliant diamond
For the first time

Now imagine that this is something
That you
And only you can see
And all that you have are words
Words you yourself can not seem to find
To try to show these things to others
So that they might be able to understand
Just how beautiful they truly are

A blessing at times
A curse at others
In so many ways
This is genius

Ed Roberts 12/20/07

A Flame Lost

I am upset today
The sun is not shining
Winter's breath is blowing
There's another storm on the way

The world itself
Is a little bit colder
A light
A single flame
Went out this morning
The news spread quickly

Benazir Bhutto
Is dead

It's a world away
From my small home
Here in Oklahoma
I never met her
She had no clue
Who I am
But like so many others
I feel her loss

She dared to stand up
Against those in power
Against the social
And gender classes around her
She tried to make things better
Tried to build a better world around her
For those who have yet
To be born

Hate took her away today
A bomber
Blinded by men who refuse to let go
Men who want things to stay the same

The man that did this today
Was merely a tool
A weapon against change
Fired from some office of power
By men too cowardly
To stand and fight for themselves

Yes
I am upset today
And I will allow my heart
To feel a few hours of grief
Allow my soul to shed the tears
It needs to
To survive
And then tomorrow
I shall once again put on my armor
Grab my strongest pen and paper
And step back out into this world
To fight

We can make a difference
Things really can change
They can extinguish flames
Here and there
But the fire of hope
And freedom

The true pillar we all carry inside
Of love
Can not
And will not be allowed
To smolder into darkness

Not as long as there is a single match to light
And a single person left here among us
That has the courage
To dream

We will miss you
Benazir Bhutto

Rest assured
You will not be forgotten

Ed Roberts 12/27/07

The Line of Life

We swat a fly
Step on an ant
Without remorse

We trap a mouse
Poison a rat
We view them as a pest
Kill them
Any chance we get

Many go out of their way
To kill a spider or a snake
By any means
We see them as a threat

We cry at the passing of a dog
Or cat
But lead thousands of cattle
And pigs
To slaughter each day

Sometimes I stop to wonder
At what point
Is a single life precious
Where exactly is the line
Where we are to be concerned
With its passing

Tonight I sit here
Alone at my computer
And ask myself
This not-so-simple question
And fear
That maybe
There should be
No such line at all

Am I not
But a single life
Myself

Ed Roberts 5/18/06

Slavery

Slavery knows no color
No religion
It cares not
Man, woman
Or child

It is born from need
And perpetuated by
Greed
And disregard
For the value of another

It stains our past
Brother selling brother
Parents selling children
The powerful
Caging the weak
The rich
Shackling the poor

In the shadows
Even today
It lives

Far from the sight of the civilized
Children still toil
Men and women
Far from their homes
Labor for food and water
And consider themselves
The lucky ones
For they are not left to starve
With all the rest

Slavery knows no color
No race
No religion
It stains our past
Haunts our todays
And looms in all of our futures

Into its arms
We sell ourselves
Everyday

Everyday
We sit idly by
And deny its very existence

Ed Roberts 4/09/06

Where does poetry come from

Where does poetry come from
A simple and very complex question

From life
From your heart
From your soul
From all around you
From deep inside you
From somewhere that you could never explain

When does poetry come

When you least expect it
When you are all alone
When you are in the middle of a crowd
When you can not find a pen
Never when you want it to

How much does poetry cost

Poetry is free
Sometimes it costs you everything
And more

How much does poetry pay

Nothing
Sometimes more than you could ever imagine

Why write poetry

Because you enjoy it
To help yourself
To help others
To change the world
Because you really have no other choice
Because you have to breathe

What is poetry

Words that rhyme
Words that don't
Sometimes something greater than the words on the
page
All that you have left to show for your tears
Life itself

Ed Roberts 2/11/08

The Purpose of You

Your body is
65% oxygen
18% carbon
10% hydrogen
3% nitrogen
1.5% Calcium

Several other chemicals and minerals
Make up the remaining 2.5%

One could buy these elements
Order them from a factory someplace
And do so
For about one dollar and seventy five cents
Give or take a bit for inflation
That is

Broken down to its basic elements
You are worth this
And no more

You are however
A one-of-a kind
A masterpiece of God's creation
The one and only
You

There was none other
Before you
The will be no other
After you are gone

You can not be
Replaced

Everything on this Earth
Has a purpose
Everything has value

There are times
When all of us feel worthless
All of us
Feel broken
Worth only as much
As these chemicals
That I listed before

Still
God himself chose to put these things together
For a reason

It is up to each of us
To try our best to discover
Just what this purpose
Is
Before once again
To these basic elements
We do return

Ed Roberts 6/01/07
(For Martha)

Each moment of life is precious
A gift that can not be replaced

We all need a dream

We all need a dream
Something we can wake up to
Inspire us to get out of bed
Something we can carry with us
Carry inside
When we step outside into this harsh world

A dream can have many shapes
It could be a place
Some distant shore
Upon which we dream of placing our feet

It could be a thing
A big house
A new car
Who knows
Maybe even both

A dream might be measurable
So many dollars and cents in the bank
So much land
That we can call our own

It might be abstract
Something that can only be measured from within
To me
These are special
Yes, my kind of dreams

We can keep our dreams to ourselves
Share them with others
And in some special cases
Make someone else's dream come true
For them

We all do need a dream
Something that we can wake to
In the end
It might really be all that simple
Because even waking
For some
Might be a dream come true

Ed Roberts 12/10/06

Seeing the World

I see with my ears
I hear each and every breath you take
From your nose or through your mouth
I hear the wind as it moves across the treetops
The raindrops as they fall to the ground
I can hear a child laugh
From nearly one hundred yards away
I also can hear their tears
Each and every sob of their pain
I can tell a lie from the truth
Simply by the tone of your voice
No, your skin doesn't get in the way
All I hear is your heart
I see all of this
With my ears

I see with my skin
I see the sun
By feeling its warmth upon my face
I see lightning
By the way it makes the hairs on my arms
Stand out straight
I see your face
By a single touch of my hands
I see walls
By the change in temperature
The dark ones are warmer
Don't you know
Yes, I see with my skin

I see with my nose
I can tell you where flowers are growing
What kind they are by their scent

I can tell you when the milk is bad
The bread is molding
What cologne you like to wear
What shampoo you used this morning
And even if you skipped your shower
You always use way too much deodorant
If you have to dress in a hurry
I can tell you when the biscuits are done
The coffee pot is about to go dry

I can even tell you how far away the bus is right now
Even though it is still around the corner
You might not fully understand
But I do see with my nose

All of these things
I see each and every day
I know my eyes don't work anymore
Believe me
There isn't a moment that passes
That I wish somehow that they would
But this is something I learned to deal with
So many years ago
I see so much of this world
That so many people simply take for granted
Some things they will never be aware of
But somehow
Just because I no longer have the use of my eyes
They all consider me
To be the one
Who is blind

Ed Roberts 7/14/07

197

The Sea of Things

It's his birthday
He stares impatiently at the stack of boxes
Each wrapped in paper with such care
He hurries through his cake and ice cream
Not taking the time to savor their flavor
In the end it's all about the presents
That is what everyone came for

They circle in anticipation
He sits in the center
Viciously unwraps each one
Another movie
Another car
Another jacket
Another this
Another that

In five minutes it's all over
Piles of paper on one side
A stack of things on the other
He walks around the room giving
"Thank You' kisses and hugs

Fifteen minutes later
Everyone is gone
Father and mother start to clean up the remains
Papers are placed in the waste basket
Half-drank punch glasses are poured down the sink
What's left of the cake is placed in the refrigerator
All is back the way it was before

One by one
He carries his new "Treasures" to his room
Finds a place to lay them
On the floor amongst the others
Each now simply a piece of clutter
Something for him to trip over or step on
In the middle of the night

Yes
He plays with one of them occasionally
When one happens to catch his eye
Some though simply lay there
Like they have for days, weeks, and months
A mere drop in this sea of things

Ed Roberts 12/12/06

Whose Side?

Whose side am I on
A question I am asked
Far too often
I might add

Am I
Pro-life
Or Pro-choice

Could a person really be Anti-life
And what is there is no choice
I wonder what any of you would do
If you find yourself in that situation

Am I for
Or against the War

Would anyone be Pro-war
An evil act that kills both combatants
And innocents alike
I know some wars are necessary
But I myself
Could never say I favor them over peace

Am I Republican
Democrat
A Liberal
Or a Conservative

Can anyone really tell me the difference
Liberal used to be new and innovative
Conservative meant cautious and steady minded
There is value in both you know

Whose side am I on
You ask

I am on the side
Of the hungry
The jobless
The innocent
The victims
Children
The sick
The elderly
The defenseless
The poor
Those caught in the middle
Of both conflict
And economic classes
That keep them at a point they barely survive

Call it what you wish
That's whose side I am on

I ask you now

Whose side are you on

Before you continue
Stop and listen to your heart
Because it is you
That must live with the answer

Not me

Ed Roberts 9/04/07

Poetry in the Desert

For over eight months
The mother pronghorn
Held her baby safe
Inside

The full moon rose
And with it
Came the night
That this would have to change

Away from the others
She fought
Struggled
To her last ounce of strength
And in a moment of wonder
A new life was born

Dropped
So frail
So vulnerable
Upon the sands of the desert
The single fawn
Struggled to gain its feet

In mere hours
After taking in the nourishment
Of its mother's milk
The fawn danced among the cactus
Ignorant
Of the perils that surrounded it
Waiting for a single moment
To strike

The moon slowly settled
Upon a distant horizon
The first rays
Of the soon to be scorching sun
Peered from the East

The new mother
And child
Quietly headed towards the safety
The implied safety that comes with numbers
The fellowship of the small herd

The car topped the hill
Shattering the calm that was the morning
A flash of sound
A glimpse of terror
A moment
That stretched itself
Into an eternity

The car sped on
Leaving as quickly as it had appeared
Caring not
What it left behind

The flight or flee
In the mother
Had protected her
Caught in the panic
That was the moment
She had leapt to the safety of the shoulder

In the following moments
Her heart began to realize
Her fawn had not done the same

New legs did not have the strength
New eyes
Froze the body with terror
For the fawn
The safety of the shoulder
Was simply too far from reach

In the morning's light
A mother knelt beside
Her dying fawn
Trying with her all her might
To urge her single child
Back to its feet
Knowing in her heart
That the damage done
Was far too great

The sun rose upon the small body
The sky filled with buzzards
That circled
Waiting for their feast

A lone car slows
Along a desolate stretch of highway
And comes to a stop
Beside the small delicate corpse

A tear fights its way out
Soon followed by others
And a simple man struggles
Through the emotions left behind
As the mother disappears
Quickly through a barbed wire fence

God
He pleads

Where did I leave my pen?

Ed Roberts 5/16/06

So many people drive by without seeing a thing.
Some do catch a glimpse
But leave feeling nothing.
I hope that you can understand
That there are times that I pray
That I could be one of those people.
There are
Of course
Times that I fall to my knees
And thank God in Heaven
That I am not.
To me
Life is really poetry
And in so many ways
Poetry itself
Is truly life.

The Criminal

By law
He is a criminal
Wanted by the police for committing a felony

In their eyes
He is a kidnapper

He did try things their way
First however
He went through the court system
Paid attorneys all he had
To fight for justice

He stood in front of the judge
Told him about his and his former wife's past
How his life had changed
How hers hadn't

He showed the judge pictures
Different men
Coming in and leaving the house
At all hours of the night
The same house
Where his five-year-old daughter slept
Yes, he showed the judge a lot of pictures

He showed the judge
Drug paraphernalia
Empty syringes
Burned spoons
Even a small bag of pills
That he had pulled from the trash
Yes, he showed the judge this as well

He told the judge
That he had moved in with his mother
Together they could provide his daughter
A safe home
More love than she had ever known
A future away from the dangers
She now faced each and every day
Yes, he told the judge
All of this

The judge listened
And made his ruling

A child belongs with its mother
He said
She was making almost twice in a month than he
was
Financially, she was far better prepared
To be the child's care giver

In the end it didn't matter
That she was a stripper at a club
That she made her money both at work
And at home
It didn't matter about the drugs
Or the alcohol

In the end
It all came down to money
Money she had
Money he didn't

He found himself facing a decision
He could either end the life of his former wife
Something he could never do
Or take his only daughter with him
And run

Now
They call him a criminal

Ed Roberts 7/24/07

I used to call him my friend
Now
I call him a man who loved his daughter enough
To leave everything behind
Just to try and keep her safe

There should never be a crime in that

Before he left
I gave him the money from my wallet
And promised to find a new home for their dog

Sometimes in life
We find ourselves faced with some tough decisions
I could not argue with the one
That he finally made

Both he and his daughter
Still hold a special place
In my prayers

Tragedy Within Arms' Reach

He lay there
Wearing his trench coat.
You could still see
The faded snowmen and snowflakes
Of the thin red blanket
The one he had picked up at a thrift store
That he tried hard to cover his body with
Each night.

He lay there
At the foot of a small oak tree
Two feet away from the sidewalk
Within arms' reach
Of the people that now passed him by.

It was two o'clock in the afternoon.
People would shake their head
As they scurried on.

"Get a job"
One man uttered
In not so soft of a voice.

"Try not to stare"
One woman warned her children
As she hurried them along their way.

He just lay there by the sidewalk
Ignoring them all
Paying them no notice
Letting them go about their everyday routine.

He lay there at six o'clock
As many left their jobs
And started their daily trek home
"Wasn't he here this morning?"
One man thought
As he hurried to catch the bus.
"No, it couldn't be him"
He assured himself
"These bums all look alike."

He lay there
All that evening
The next day
And the next

Tightly wrapped in his thrift store blanket
Wearing his dark black trench coat
Two feet away from the sidewalk
Under a small oak tree
He lay there
And no one stopped to notice
That he had frozen to death
Several nights before.

He lay there
A frozen tragedy
And all this time
Two feet away from a sidewalk
Easily within so many arms' reach.

Such a sad tale
You might sigh to yourself.

What you must realize
What you must force yourself to understand is
This is not a simple poem.

This was yesterday.
This was Paris.

I wonder
How many other cities
Could this have been as well?

Ed Roberts 11/29/05

The Bottom

Have you ever lied
To someone you loved
Swore to them on your very life
That you were clean
Praying that they couldn't tell
That you had a bottle of pills
In your coat pocket

Have you ever
Picked up a needle off the ground
And jabbed it into your arm
Not caring where it had been
Not knowing who had used it last
The only thing that mattered
Is that there was 3 CC's
Of something left inside
That might get you high

Have you ever puked your guts out
Because you've downed two bottles
Of dollar mouth wash
And prayed the buzz would kick in
Before you had to down anymore

Have you ever left your child
Your baby
Alone in a car seat
While you went inside the bar
To get your next drink
Not even stopping to pay attention
That it was 100 degrees outside

Have you ever offered your body
To someone who the very sight of
Made you want to vomit
Simply because you knew
They had a little bag
Of what you needed most

Have you ever woke up
Naked and alone
Laying in a pool of vomit and piss
And the only thing you could think of
Was where you were going to make
Your next score

You think you have hit bottom
You think things could not possibly get worse

Believe me
They can

Get help
Now

Ed Roberts 12/18/07

213

The Greatest Poet in the World

The greatest poet in the world
At night
Sleeps at the homeless center
Downtown
He has seen so many people's faces
Heard all their stories
Everyday he sees life in so many colors
From so many different angles
And in his spare moments
Those between finding something to eat
And shelter from the world
He lives poetry
For all those that will listen
The saddest part of all is
He has never learned
How to write

The second greatest poet in the world
Spends her waking hours
In a nursing home
For nearly ninety years
She has survived on this planet
Countless times
She has fallen in love
Made love
Lost love
And found the strength to start anew
Her hands no longer can hold a pen
She never learned to operate a computer
No
She has been around far longer than they have
She sits in her wheelchair
And recites her life story

Sometimes to others
Sometimes to herself
The saddest part of all
No one cares to write it down

The third greatest poet in the world
Records his work with paper and pen
Places each poem neatly in a folder
Which he stacks amongst the others
That he keeps upon a shelf
He writes before he goes to work
He writes when he can between customers
And sometimes he writes
When he gets back home
The saddest part of all
Is that the third greatest poet on this planet
Sells cars to make a living
He dreams someday
That someone will find and understand his work
Long after he is gone

The fourth greatest poet in the world
Is only nine
He lives in Iraq
And writes whenever he can find a pencil and paper
The saddest part of all
Is that he will never live to see ten

Here I give you
The top four poets in the world
No, you may never know their names
No, you may never see their faces
The saddest part of all
Is that you might not ever get to know
The fifth or the sixth
Either

Poetry is life
Life is poetry
Sometimes to write it
To be able to appreciate it to its fullest
First one must live it
And in the end
They take it with them
Only if we are lucky
Do they leave a small piece of it
Behind

Ed Roberts 5/17/07

I thought it would be harder

I remember the day clearly
The day I took my first drink
We snuck a bottle of Jim Beam
Billy and me
From the liquor cabinet
Of a friend's parent's house
We thought it would somehow make us feel
Grownup
Cool
It just made me sick

I thought it would be a lot harder
To take that second drink
It wasn't

I remember the day clearly
The day I bought my first joint
I bought it from another kid at school
I smoked it
Yes, with Billy
In the field not far from home
We thought it would make us feel good
Cool again
I didn't really feel much at all

I thought it would be a lot harder
To smoke that second joint
It wasn't
The sad part is
I never felt any better
After I smoked it as well

I somewhat remember
When I decided to try something a little stronger
I'm not sure exactly where it was I started
We started
Billy and I
I just know there were pills
And pipes
We tried anything
And everything
There always seemed to be something new

Of course
Nothing came without a price
None of this stuff is free you know

I remember clearly the day
The first time I robbed a man for cash
I was actually shaking more than he was
He dropped his wallet and ran

I thought it would be harder
To rob another person at gun point
It wasn't
Not until something went wrong

We decided
Billy and I
To try our hand at robbing a convenience store
They always were busy
Should always have plenty of cash
What we didn't know
Was that behind the counter
They also kept a shotgun

Everything happened so fast
The man behind the counter
Opened the register
Spilled some change on the floor
When he came up though
He was holding the gun instead
Billy was standing in front
The force of the shot knocked both of us back
I was able to get back up to my feet
Billy never did

I thought it would be harder
To point my pistol at the head of the man
Behind the counter
I thought it would be harder to pull the trigger
To shoot a person
For the first time
It wasn't

That was all a few years ago
Now my life
If you want to call it that
Stretches from one side of this eight-by-ten cell
To the other
Each day
Is pretty much like the day before

I thought it would be harder
To end my own life
In a way
It was

But each step simply got easier
Along the way

Every road is filled with exits
Sometimes we just don't see them
Until we pass them by
Or it is simply
Way too late

Ed Roberts 1/23/06

Sometimes I write using the eye's of another. The eyes I borrowed this time were those of a young man, only twenty-five years old, that just received a sentence of life without the possibility of parole for a murder he committed during a robbery. I felt his story was one that more people needed to hear.

The Fear of Ed

The person I fear the most on this planet
Is Ed

It seems he is always there
No matter what I do
From him
There is no escape

I run
Ed finds me

I hide
Eventually he shows up

In my waking hours
In my dreams
Even in my nightmares
Ed is there

No
I know that he's human
A man just like me
I know
If I really had to
If it came right down to it
One on one
Against him I might stand a chance
But you see
He doesn't work that way

With Ed
It is always far worse

At my finest hour
Ed is there
The first one to remind me
Nothing in this world will last

At my darkest moment
Ed is there too
He's the first to make sure I know
That somehow
I brought this upon
Myself

Ed tells me
That I do not matter
He always reminds me
I am just one man
An insignificant voice
A small speck upon a giant planet
Ed does this without being asked
He does this all the time

Ed is always the one
The first one there to tell me
That no matter what I do
I can not make a difference
No matter how much I try
The world would be a much better place
And I would be a whole lot happier
If I could learn somehow
To simply sit down and shut up

Yes
This is how Ed puts things
Each and every time

You'd think
Over time
That I'd learn not to listen

You'd think
I'd get tired of Ed
And find the guts to tell him to go away
And stay the Hell away from me
Forever

Over time
You'd think I'd find some way
To get away from Ed
Somehow

But you see I'm afraid of Ed
And no matter how hard I try to convince myself
Deep down my greatest fear
Is that in the end
Ed is right

Ed Roberts 6/30/07

Just Hit Play

You press
Start

The game begins

You pick off targets
One by one

They bleed
They scream
Then
They die

You move up a level
After so many kills

You stop to reload

You know how many hits
That you can take

You move ahead
Slowly

Count how many rounds
You have left

You step into an ambush
Got to remember it's here next time

You watch your life meter running low
Got to try and make it to the next level

Too late
You take a lucky hit
From your blind side

The screen turns red
Everything fades before your eyes

Game over

Once more
You die

You click on
Play again

The whole thing starts over
Once more

A voice to your left
Demands your attention

Your down time is over
Got to move on

You slide the game
Back into your pack

You
And your squad
Fan out

Slowly advance down the sidewalks

Suddenly
The air is filled with bullets
An ambush

On what is supposed to be
Friendly soil
You take out the two to your left

Your buddy takes the three
To the right

Before the last drops
He scores a lucky shot

Your friend drops
To his knees
At your feet

You reach for
Start

You beg for play over

His blood stains your boots red

You take a hit
From your blind side

You watch as your life meter
Runs low

Your screen
Fades to crimson

And you fall

Game over

Somewhere
A thousand miles away

A man sits behind his desk

Scratches his head
As he counts the casualties

He hits reload

Moves in another battalion

And once again

Hits play

Ed Roberts 4-18-06

Mercy

There is a man in Kenya
Trying to make his way home from work
He turns the wrong corner
Into a strange neighborhood he wanders
Maybe it's the color of his skin
Maybe it's his dialect
To the people living there
He is their enemy
Someone to hate

They come out of their house
They beat him with machetes
Hack him to death
Piece by piece

He begs them to stop
Pleads for his life
But his words fall upon ears
That can not understand
One simple word
Mercy

A boy from Wisconsin
Out of school for the holidays
Visits his relatives in Chicago

He goes to the mall
Decides to try and find a last minute gift
To give his Aunt and Uncle
Who were kind enough
To open their home to him

He doesn't realize his jacket
Is the wrong color
He doesn't know on whose turf
This mall belongs
It is cold
This is the only coat he owns

They stop their cars
Three of them
He doesn't see the gun pointed
Out the back window
He just feels the burning
As the bullet pierces his chest
The roar of the pistol
Is the last thing that he hears

They kick his body
As he lays there at their feet
They remember
How many of their friends have fallen
They show each other
They can have power over another
The one thing that they have forgotten
Is Mercy

Two people
A world apart
Die the same day
Both at the wrong place
At the wrong time

Both innocent
Both condemned
Killed in the place of another
Victims
Simply because they were there at hand
And I sit here trying to find something I can offer
To both the innocent and the guilty
For they themselves
Are not fully the ones to blame
And the best that I can find
Is just one word
That so many can not seem to comprehend

Mercy

Ed Roberts 1/09/08

The Businessman

Yes, I make the bombs
I put them together
With my own hands
I do this
For the money
If I did not do it
Someone else would

I don't ask
For what purpose the bomb is needed
I don't need to know these things
I am a businessman
A professional
Nothing more
Nothing less

I give money to the hungry
I give money to schools
I even give money to the Church
In their eyes
My hands are clean

You look at me
With disgust
You hate my very name
I ask you but one question
In the end
How clean are your hands

Ed Roberts 3/17/08

A Dream of Heaven

What if next year
We built no new cars
And gave those that build them
Time to make them
Better for our planet

What if next month
We built no more guns
No more bombs
No more weapons of death
What if we built implements of peace
Built schools
Hospitals
And houses
Instead

What if next week
We simply ate two meals a day
And gave the "extra" food
To those that today
Do not receive
One

What if tomorrow
We wake
And concentrate on saving the Earth
Instead of on
How to kill each other
What if we practiced our own faith
And allowed our brothers
To do the same

What if tonight
We all spent our hours of sleep
Dreaming of what it would be like
To awaken in Heaven
And when we wake
Do our best to make our tomorrow
Simply a dream come true

Ed Roberts 7/24/06

Trying to Understand the Bombing

I see you standing there
in the middle of the crowd.
You, with the cord in your hand.

Yes,
I know what it is you are carrying.
I know what it is that fills your belt.

No one else here can hear Me.
No one else can hear what you say to Me either.
For this moment
You are as invisible as you wish.

Before you pull the cord
I needed to take a few seconds to ask

Why?

What is it that brought you here?
Led you to this moment?

Was it money?
How much did they pay you for your soul?
Do you think money will buy you forgiveness?
If you do
you are a fool indeed!

Was it fame?
Do you think others will praise you?
Look around,
see all the others that will die around you.

Know now
your name upon their families lips
will be a curse until the end of time.
Is this the fame you seek?

Do you think you will be rewarded?
Is that it?
For what?
Killing innocence?
Killing children?
Rest assured you will be punished!
Rewarded, I don't think so.

Is it hate that brought you here?
Hate for whom?
From whom?
Do you hate those standing around you?
Hate the ones that will mourn at their graves?
Is this really your hate at all?

Did someone else give this to you?
Why then are you the one here?
If truly this was their belief
would not they be standing here
with the belt around their waist?
Would not the cord be in their hand instead?

I know that I could stop you.
Leave your body
like so much ash upon the floor
but I promised long ago
to let you decide your fate
and your destiny.

Do both of us a favor now.
I know that you are going to pull the cord.
I can not change your path now
and I know you understand this as well.

The favor I ask is simple,
One I have asked of others in your shoes.

With your very last breath
please,
do not with your last words
call out My name.

It is not Me that awaits you!
I promise you
you will never see Me
or hear from Me again.

Forever!

I see you there.
The one leaving the package
at the side of the road.

Now it is time
for you and Me to have a talk

Ed Roberts 11/26/05

Words from the Edge

There are so many things
That I wish I could tell you
So many words left here in my heart
That I wish I could share
But
No matter how hard I try
They remain hidden
Buried too deep
For my pen to find

I walk away
An empty shell
Broken to my very soul
Tears soak the floor beneath my feet
The only thing that is certain
Is that my heart must have time to heal

I lie here in the darkness
At the very edge of a much needed sleep
But the words they are now calling
Taking shape before my half-closed eyes
And with my last ounce of strength
I reach for the pen and paper on the nightstand
And once again
I write

Ed Roberts 3/20/08

I Thought I Knew How Much

I thought I knew
How much she loved me

We were married for forty years
We had two children together
Fine young men they are now

Yes
I thought I knew
How much she loved me

And even when the cancer came
Attacked her body in ways you can not imagine
She still held my hand
You'd have thought I was the one who was dying
She was there for me
Until her time here was done

Yes
I thought I knew
How much she loved me

It was just yesterday
I found it there
Hidden away in the back of her closet
A small box
Filled with a bundle of letters
All wrapped with a single red ribbon

I read through each of these
Letters with words filled with such emotion
They spoke of nights of wonder
Stolen moments of pleasure

And dreams of a lifetime of happiness
Yes
I thought I knew
How much she loved me

Each letter I read
Even when the tears blocked my eyes
Even when my body shook
I read each and every letter
And then
And only then
Did I truly understand

Here she had kept this box of letters
Precious memories
Words filled with such passion
And not a single one of these
Were mine

Now
I understand just how much she loved me
Because she had him
And all of these wonderful letters
Yet, married me instead

God
I miss her so much

Ed Roberts 3/8/08

That Someone

There are those out there
That will tell you
No matter what you do
Things are destined to always get worse

No matter how hard you try
In the end
There will be
Hell on Earth

There is nothing that you
A single person
Can do to change this
This is what is meant to be

My answer to this is simple
They are wrong

They have already accepted defeat
Yes, in the end
They will lose this battle
Accepting their path
Is merely to surrender to doom itself

When the days have reached their darkest
When hope itself
Has been squeezed to its last ounce
There will have to be someone
Someone left to stand against the storm
Someone to bring back the light
That is found in all of us

I realize my time here is short
I know that I could never be that person
This is why I leave these words here
For you

Take these words
Reach deep into your very soul
And
Do the one thing so many will fear

Be that someone

Ed Roberts 12/14/07

There is one more poem written by my friend and brother Chase Von. With his pen and his heart he is changing the world both as a writer and publisher.

241

With His Pen

The words
That pour forth from your soul
Can be likened to food
That a starving people
Are stumbling upon...
Perhaps your greatest gift
Is your inability to completely accept
You are gifted...
Fear is only useful for fight or flight
Your words are being eaten and absorbed
Like manna
If you, which I know you won't
Were to succumb to that fear
Think of how many searching
For the logic and sensibility
They are craving
That you provide
Would starve or worse still
Feed upon other things????

You have far more power than you know
It doesn't happen often but in this instance
It has been placed most assuredly
In the right hands
The hands of a Warrior

A Warrior
Who unselfishly
Feeds the starving
By hunting and sharing what he traps
With his pen

Chase Von 12/15/05
(Written for and about Ed Roberts)

Please visit his web site
http://www.webspawner.com/users/chasevon/

Once again I leave the pen on the table

*There are so many without whom I could not have
taken this so far*

Words can never repay the support

The love

And the guidance they have given me

I thank God everyday I do not wield this pen alone

I give a special thanks to

Ursula T. Gibson (She went above and beyond in helping put this book together)

George Manos (A very skilled writer and poet in his own right)

&
Chase Von (A man I look to more as a brother than a friend, even though we have never met.)

These people act both as editors and friends
(Some would argue one could not be both)

Of course without my mother Wanda
Many errors and misspelled words would have made it through as well

Without my wife Letha
I would not be here
Her love is more important than the air I breathe

Our two sons
Adam and Alex are now men to be proud of
And our grandchildren
Noah and Caina
Are our hope for the future

Finally I wish to thank you
The reader
For without you
My life as a writer
Would truly have no purpose at all

About the Author

Ed Roberts – father, son, grandfather, writer, poet, publisher, and works for a major car rental company. At 49, Ed is a man that enjoys sharing all of these roles, sometimes in the same day. He was born and raised in Oklahoma City, Oklahoma.

This along with his American Indian heritage has had a great influence on his writing.

His first book "A Poet's Last Stand' was released September, 2002.

He released his second book "I'm Still Standing" on CD in Adobe Acrobat format December of 2003.

His third book "Everything Must Have a Beginning, a Middle, and an End" was released in September of 2005.

He has had poems appear in The Poetry Sharings Journal, poems and articles in Poetic Voices Magazine, and poetry posted on many different web sites around the world, many in other languages.

Ed is a member of both the Academy of American Poets and the Poetry Society of Oklahoma.

He is the founder, writer, and publisher of the books that make up the Poetry For Life Project.

The goal of this project is to help those dealing with major problems in life including drug and alcohol abuse, abuse in the family, suicide, and the loss of family members.

"Poetry can be a lot more than mere words on a sheet of paper. There are times in all of our lives where we need special words to deal with this thing we call life. Poetry can be these words we are looking for."

Books by Ed Roberts

A Poet's Last Stand*
I'm Still Standing*
*Everything Must Have a Beginning, a Middle,
and an End**

To see poetry videos by Ed Roberts visit
http://www.youtube.com/user/amayhem11

For more poetry please visit
www.edrobertspoetry.com

Other Books Published by
Von Chase Publishing

Paradox
tin hearts
and
Vanity

Also see these books by Chase Von

Pink, Blue, and Green
Your Chance To Hear The Last Panther Speak

(With the 2nd and 3rd book I included a special poem after which I shared comments left on my poetry site by readers. I wrote this poem today so that I might be able to do the same with this one as well.)

Ink in the Storm

Deep within my soul
The ink is mixed
Churned by a storm
That threatens the very fabric
Of my being

I am left with little choice
I wait
I pray for strength
I long for release
And in the end
Hope for survival

Usually at the point
Of my last ounce of strength
The very moment of my last breath
The very edge of my own existence
The words come

Often upon a simple piece of parchment
A tear-soaked canvas of white
They burn themselves from my pen
Scorching all of me in their path

These are not my words
The ones you see before you

I am merely the tool
The pen in the hand of another
One who left these words here now
For you

For you to use if you need
Share if you desire
Carry with you along your path of life
Or leave here upon this page
If you choose

My part in this is finished
I sit alone in the darkness to heal
Awaiting the next coming storm
And watching

As the words spread from one page to the next
One heart to the next
And if I am lucky I get to listen
Listen to the whispers of their souls

Listen softly
For my words here are done
And I leave you here now
With theirs

Ed Roberts 07/05/08

Now here are words written by so many others -

2006-07-07 01:29:10
A poem written By the Man who left the Bar
Mr. Roberts, Ed, I have spent the last ten years of my life teaching others what is and what is not poetry. I have preached rules, different writing techniques, and basically tried to educate those that would pay attention to this wonderful craft. I have spent the last hour on your site reading all that you have posted here. You exhibit little knowledge of the rules of poetry and you maintain no specific style. If I were to try to grade you on form or method I am afraid you would fail. Still in this last hour you my friend have left me nothing short of speechless. Never have I seen a writer capable of literally reaching into one's soul and painting images there that will last a lifetime. What troubles me most is how would anyone ever hope to try and instruct someone on how to write in the manner? I leave here with eyes that have been cried dry, a few scribbled notes to mull over later, and an entirely new perspective on just how powerful poetry can be. Rest assured, when I have had time to recover I will come here again.

2006-06-30 12:34:37
A poem written By the Man who left the Bar
My God this is so powerful. I lost my brother five years ago in a car accident. You'd think that would have reached me, huh? Let me assure this has!!!!!!!!!!!!!!!!!!!! I will never be that man, with a single poem you sobered me up to try and be the man my brother would have been proud of.

249

2006-06-18 08:58:15
Elmo's Poem
I have read this one before. I completely relate to it, because my nephew was also special.
He died when he was 5 and everyone told my sister, "Well, at least, he is happy now."
She responded that he was happy here, because he didn't know any better. An awesome and touching write.

2006-06-12 22:49:42
I Used to Have a Brother Once
I have a friend. A friend who was strung out and violent until she got so violent and strung out she killed a man. I have a friend who spent years and years in prison until she met my other friend. The friend I had before her. Now my friend is a whole new person. She's peaceful and compassionate, oh yea... and she's drug free. She turned out to be such a good friend, I married her and together we've grown to realize that the only option is choice and the only guarantee is that one day, your choice for forgiveness and too forgive, will surely, run out. I'm glad my friend and I chose wisely. I pray you and your brother will too. Peace.

2006-05-31 08:35:21
A poem written By the Man who left the Bar
Ed--This is a horrifying work...to have to life with that!!!!--I know accidents happen but some accidents are promoted by substances that shouldn't have been there while operating a car--I know a woman who this happened to and she can NEVER forgive herself!!!

--But, unfortunately, accidents do happen--There comes a time when we all must forgive and move on...hard as that is to do!!!-- GREAT job here....filled with emotion

2006-05-26 07:55:35
I`ll See You Later
Now you really got me crying Ed. There are a few more poems on this list but I can barely breathe right now. What you give us is so much more than poetry. You share with us your heart and soul.
I understand why God himself chose to leave you with us a while longer.
WE NEED YOU HERE SO BADLY!!!!!!!!!!!!!!! I can never say goodbye to my son. I'll see you later is not easy either.

2006-05-26 07:48:53
There was a Man
Tomorrow would have been my son Robert thirteenth birthday. He was killed by a drunk driver March 28th. The saddest part of all is that the boy driving the car that struck him was only 17 himself. I plan on getting involved with MADD to help try and keep more mothers from being in this position. My friend Betty gave me a list of your poems that she said I had to read. I know why she chose this one.

2006-05-25 22:59:22
Where Will You Be After
Wow!!! As a recovering alcoholic I can sooooo relate! Excellent poem very powerful!

2006-05-25 02:40:17
Where Will You Be After

This is such a brilliant show of emotion. I myself for a while was dependant on drink...but that pinpoints the amount of dangers it can lead to, I am sad to say I have experienced most of them... a great write

2006-05-22 22:06:53
Missing
Today marks the one year anniversary of my daughter Kimberly's death. I was what was missing in her life, a life she took on her 16th birthday. Now she is missing in mine. Your words tear my heart apart like no other I have EVER read.
You don't know how hard I pray that I could have read them earlier. I have read several of your poems tonight.
You helped me in more ways than I could ever say. Bless you and I hope these words find more dads that need them. Hopefully before it is too late for them.

2006-05-21 01:10:34
I`ll See You Later
I took your advice and read some of your poetry. This one touched me the most. I have lost so many people close to me in my short life and I find it so hard to say good bye. It's so rough when you don't want to... good bye just seems so ... permanent. "I'll See You Later"... I like it. Thank you.

2006-05-20 14:55:11
5 Single Words
As a disabled person due to a terrible accident, I suffered a stroke at the early age of 48 yrs. It has left me paralyzed on my right side, confined to w/chair, unable to walk, without assistance. That was 6 yrs. ago! I woke up from an 8 wk. coma, with most of my

252

memory lost. There were times I came close to the end!..But we are survivors! God has been so merciful!!....thanks so much for sharing, as I can relate perfectly to this poem!...Very true & well written!...I really enjoy reading your writings!...best wishes for your success!

2006-05-10 20:09:28
Tears of a Monster
This poem touched me to the core of my being, heart wrenching, excellently written, I know how you must feel, My husband and I adopted a 16 yr. old cat from an animal shelter, 3 months. ago, he had a look of such hopelessness in his old eye's and we new his chance of being adopted was slim to nothing,
He now is bright eyed and loves affection, I love animals so much and It's evident you do too,
God bless you and stop beating yourself up, as much as we would like to we can't save them all
2006-05-08 08:42:01
They Didn't Know
Touching story of a boy who could have made a difference but chose not to.
We can never change what we do or what we could have done. That stays with us until we can forgive ourselves.....ouch....sometimes we simply can't even do that. Nicely written with an imagery all to clear.

2006-05-08 08:34:46
Tears of a Monster
Tears come to my eyes while reading this. For we are only a monster if we deem ourselves to be. Doing what we must is sometimes uncomfortable and we can hold ourselves to blame for our actions but if it is necessary to do, then it can be twice as bad in our minds because we really don't want to do

253

*what we must. Tormented emotions here as the
visionary within this poem is all too surreal!! Great
job! and sorry for the loss of a dearly loved animal.*

2006-04-27 06:32:10
The Hands of God
*Fantastic! I heard a minister say recently, "Look
around you. When two or three are gathered ...there
the Lord will be ~ Feel Him as He moves between us
while we sit and pray in this church." And it struck
me that the Lord doesn't move between us... He
moves within us. He's not between you and me; He
IS you and me... and the unwed mother, and the
man with aids, and the father of five who's just been
laid off, the addict, the pornography watcher, the
policeman and soldier.
He's the banker and lawyer... the child, the
grandmother who has to decide between medicines
and utility bills in the dead of winter. Your work
evokes powerful images, my friend. God bless you
always*

2006-04-22 23:52:52
There was a Man
*You wrote this on my birthday! My father is an
alcoholic. You make me feel close to reality. I love it!
All of it. I have never let anyone around me drink
and drive. I know what you stand for and it's
powerful. You're truly gifted. Now I'm afraid I've said
too much.*

2006-04-20 23:04:52
Death of a Child hood
*Damn this was hard, straight at my face. You want to
be a player, be cool for folks. This made me stop
and look at the bill I'm running up, written checks I*

really can't pay. This poem took me down to where I gotta be, get things back together and straighten myself back up. I always said if my momma couldn't change me, no one could. I guess I needed to run into you.

2006-04-20 17:57:42
You Let Him
Well this brought up tears and memories I thought I had left behind... I was in a similar situation where my stepdad would beat the crap out of my mom and when I tried to stop it I was in trouble for disrespecting him....well years later I married a man that I loved more than life, he broke my heart and my jaw in the same night but I left and never went back.
The really stupid thing is I still miss him and I wonder if things have changed. I know that I have seen my fair share of abuse both mental and physical but all in all what doesn't kill ya makes you stronger, after years and years of counseling (I can save you a great deal of money here....lol) I have become a survivor, I have left the victim role behind and have stood up for those who can't! Some days I believe that I went through all I did because there are those out there that god just thought couldn't handle it.
So now that you know my life story I guess to sum it up I thought this was THE most excellent well written poem I have ever read!

2006-04-15 17:39:12
Beat Me
You are a very good poet. I came from India to England to rescue my sister. Made him leave England. He went back to India to his town and died

255

there. Once he broke my sister's hand. Both bones were broken and she still has a steel rod in one bone. I feel your pain and anger. Great poem.

2006-04-15 17:34:15
There was a Man
Thank you for this poem. One of the PP poet's boyfriends was killed recent by a hit and run driver so this poem to me has much more value than other's who have not gone through similar experience. Very nicely written poem. Take care,

2006-04-15 17:25:45
Where Will You Be After
Ed I know exactly what you are talking about; I won't go into the why`s and wherefore`s. It's not easy living with someone who drinks. Good advice if only they will take it. The beer adverts are getting a bit more graphic thank goodness.

2006-04-12 21:52:07
I`ll See You Later
This is a truly beautiful poem, In my situation my grandpa slipped into a coma for his last week and we weren't aware if he could here us when we sat with him and talked, he was unresponsive. I told him some of the funny stories that I remembered and sat and cried by his side, I don't know if he knew we where there but for my grandms' sanity, I told her he could.
Who am I to say that he couldn't? He lived a good life and we were proud of him and all that he did. He may have moved to a much better place but we all keep pieces of him within us and that is what helped me through. Your poem is so heartfelt I will share

this one with my grammy and I am sure she will love it!!!!!!!! Thank You so much

2006-04-12 02:02:19
You're Not Heavy
I really love personal stories--this one is touching as well. It actually got me choked up reminding me to spend as much time possible with my grandma and other family members that are in those yrs. It also didn't help that 3/28 is my b-day. Sorry for you're loss

2006-04-12 00:15:40
My Greatest Horror (II)
we were asked to pick a poem to read for poetry month in class. our teacher wanted us to pick an important poet from the US. Most people picked poe, elliot frost, and the like. A few kids laughed when i picked this poem by you. they stopped laughing as soon as i started reading the poem. Now i'm not the only one who thinks you might be the most powerful poet to ever come from this country. Mom is ordering a copy of your book to give to the school library.
I'm sure there will be a long waiting list to read it. i wish every school would do this.

2006-04-06 22:24:38
Beat Me
My husband would totally agree.

2006-04-06 19:06:14
My Greatest Horror (II)
WOW! This is so moving. I've read this before and cried my eyes out the 1st time though the 1st time I read it

I read the original. I left feedback on it months ago. My daughter is 15 and learning about the Holocost in school right now. I came here to read this to her and found your second version (this one). She decided she wanted to print the page and take it into school to her teacher and to read for the class. With a write like this on the web... something tells me that this final horror might not be such a horror. with words and heart pouring out facts such as these. how can one deny such a powerful..

testimony. You have more strength then I've ever met in my life. Thank You for educating the world on this cruel unfair time in our history. You have such a wonderful way with words.

2006-04-04 19:30:16
I thought it would be harder
Doing 3rd year of 25 here in Calif. earned internet privileges today was surprised to see a poetry site on the list of sites GOD I wish i could've come here earlier things really might have been different will read more and let a few friends here know to come here as well Dude you are a light in a whole lot of darkness

2006-03-31 01:29:18
The Silent Voice
I think I am going to show this one to my cousin charity. I think she needs it. Great write!

2006-03-16 01:13:56
A poem written By the Man who left the Bar
I cried a river from this poem I could see myself here. God, i think of the mornings I have woken up not knowing who or where I was. This very easily could have been me. I read your other poem about

*the man that left the bar. I promise you you touched
something so deep in my soul that this will never be
me. I never liked poetry but was told by a friend I
had to come here.*
*This is so much more than the word poetry can ever
express. to me your words are a God send.*

2006-03-13 09:12:21
A Cure for the Past
*Meeting myself after a similar course was one of the
greatest rewards of my life.*

2006-03-02 14:22:59
Us vs. Them
*The question is will they know who they are? They
need to read your words. You really have the power
to change them into one of us.*

2006-02-24 14:30:49
Death of a Child hood
*I have spent an hour reading the poems here. You
made me cry more than once. It has been years
since I have been able to do that. You made me feel
again, something I had forgotten somewhere in the
past how to do. I live in a world most people dream
of, got the money, all the stuff I ever wanted, or
thought I did.*
*There is so much emptiness behind the eyes I see.
Even behind my own. You filled them with tears and
in doing so let me feel my soul again. I hope
somehow more people find out about your poetry
but I also hope it never gets to the point where you
get too much attention.*
*Of course I don't think the people in my world could
change you, you might end up shattering their world
instead. It is so rare to see a person spread out*

259

upon a page. What is more special is that in your words I see nothing but truth.

2006-02-21 13:14:36
Us vs. Them
This poems burns through you like the wind to your very bones. My cousin was killed in a bombing in Amman, they were 25 years old.
These men would have called me brother and you the enemy. I will never be one of them and will stand by your side. They damn themselves to hell with their actions. You are a lamp sent to us by God to shed light on their evil.

2006-02-09 10:47:28
I Used to Have a Brother Once
We have all had family that we have lost to the demons of life...drugs, drink. Its sad when we try to help they run away...good poem

2006-02-09 10:40:17
Udomfo Must Die
That is a description of an African child born in despair....a product of rape. unwanted by his mother and the world. Surviving against all odds...until he becomes me...inspired by poverty, war to write poetry of peace and the struggle....Udomfo will survive through the strife

2006-01-30 13:31:59
I thought it would be harder
You have a way of looking inside a person and seeing directly into their very soul. I have taken too many wrong turns on the road of life. Thank you for reminding me there are always exits to take besides that final one.

Gonna stop for a while and see if I can find the best for me to take. Your poem was like a street light I am glad I slowed down for.

2006-01-25 12:22:20
A poem written By the Man who left the Bar
The day of forgiveness for ones actions can always materialize if we can understand that we simply did not know any better!! What a powerful write and finding it hard to believe you can capture such detail without experiencing this but on the other hand so glad that is wasn't you!!
If this wasn't written from your own experience then I applaud your talent and gift to write from the reflection of another human beings dreadful experience! BUT if it truly was...then you have just shared your experience with another human being and can now start the path of forgiving...to thine own self be true!!

2006-01-17 00:17:41
Death of a Child hood
I have learned so much from your poetry. My father died when i was 6. He could have been the man in your poem There was a Man. Of course so could have I as well. That poem slapped me like nothing I had ever read, until now. I have kept a switch blade in my dresser and was thinking of buying a gun from a guy at school. with this poem you let me know the difference between being a boy and a man.
I want to be a kid a little longer, might use the hotline number to report the other guy. We don't need any more guns at school. we really need you!!!!!!!!!!!!!

2006-01-16 21:39:03
My Greatest Horror (II)

Oh my Lord... This is a powerful poem. I studied the Holocaust in school (Ramstein Germany - Air Force) and even now, I am deeply hurt over the lives lost and a thought expanded into killing and terror. This poems brings back many memories of tears I have cried for all those who have died. Peace and blessings to you,

2006-01-07 04:49:10
An Arab from Cleveland
yes this is true. I wish that everyone in the world could jsut see, that the rest of the world is no different from themselves. Being form Ohio I know the diversity of Cleveland. Here's another one for you. I am in Baghdad. The man who owns the internet cafe on my camp and several others is an Iraqi man from Michigan.
2006-01-06 18:34:50
The Value of One Life
You really caught me off guard with this poem. As I read on and on I honestly felt a little anger myself until i got to the end and found out what you were reading from. I often think of how it must of been like to be a slave, someone else's property, and it makes me sick. Great story and idea. It really made me think. You have alot of talent.

2006-01-04 03:30:37
Trying to Understand the Bombing
Sir, this poem with its words has ripped my world in two. From my childhood I was taught to hate the infidel. We were promised so many things for being loyal to their teachings. Your poem takes away the smoke they use to cloud the truth. It reaches into one's soul and makes it listen to the true voice of

Allah. I praise you for leaving this here for me to find. I pray many others will follow behind.

2005-12-30 17:20:41
They Didn`t Know
My parents have no idea of the things i have done. I may never tell them. I just wanted to tell you there will be a lot less that they will have to worry about in the future. You have really given me the slap in the face i needed.

2005-12-29 08:33:04
My Greatest Horror
Oh... Mr Roberts I am so over come that I can barely write this, tears are streaming from my eyes as I read the words that you have written...I can only say that I will never allow any one in my presence to mock the atrocities that you must have endured in your life at the hands of these monsters! Thank You for sharing your pain, so that others will perhaps understand.

2005-12-29 08:20:58
5 Single Words
I am covered with goose flesh after reading your entry here...I applaud you for you courage to continue to go on in spite of all that you are going through...we are all here for a reason, and yours is apparent to me...You inspire HOPE, in a world where things seem HOPELESS. Thank You for a very thought provoking read.

2005-12-27 13:03:16
Where Will You Be After
Very good poem! There is nothing good about one having a first drink which can lead to something

worse far worse. I never knew my grandfather because he was in a drunken stupor and committed suicide before I was born. His family lived a bad life. My grandmother had to work where she could find a job. My mother was twelve years old and had to live at various relatives homes all because her father chose to take that first drink! My husband filed for a divorce after twenty-three years because he wanted to be free,live wild, drink, and run around with women. Drinking alcoholic beverages opens the door to so much evil! You said it well in your poem!

2005-12-26 16:09:25
I`ll See You Later
We lost my mother yesterday. i have been to this site before but had never seen this poem. Thank you so much for putting it here. It brings comfort to a broken soul and makes this holiday season a bit more bearable.

2005-12-24 05:30:10
The Value of One Life
*As I read this poem, I remembered my great grand mother, who passed away about 4 yrs ago. She would have been 98 this November. Her mom died at age 106,1978, the year i was born.
I never got to meet her, but i heard stories from my great-grandmother about slavery days. It makes me respect life and the things around me. A persons life is priceless. Your poem was so beautiful.*

2005-12-23 03:25:04
Trying to Understand the Bombing :
i don't honestly know what to say about this piece...its absolutely brilliant and heart wrenching at the same time...extremely relevant and eloquent...it

also voices a lot of my personal feelings that have become stronger since one of my best friends has been deployed to iraq...and i agree, poetry isn't always free, but if you can help one person see clearly then it is worth that price...well done my friend...amazingly well done...

2005-12-15 00:30:31
Trying to Understand the Bombing
I have read and commented on a few of your poems before. You, my friend, are the voice from the desert. I still pray you will find your true place in this world. You are our hope for the future, still you hide in the shadows.
You shoes will leave ever-lasting prints on this Earth but for our sake you must step into the light before the darkness engulfs us all.

.
2005-12-03 00:28:33
Trying to Understand the Bombing
Your words here peel away the mask of lies that shrouds those taken in with promises of pleasures. I will spread these to all that will hear them.

2005-11-28 10:56:05
The Empty Room
I really enjoyed your poem. A friend of mine lost her son in an accident and leaves everything the way he left it. She says that she peeks in every night before she goes to sleep. I will have her read this
2005-11-25 19:29:44
The Way of the Cross
My brother wore a cross. He was killed in Africa last year. His death didn't even make the newspaper. Your poem gives him the tribute he deserved. You speak for all of us, many more people need to listen.

2005-11-18 00:30:59
The Value of One Life
Sir, i had family members that were bought and sold. Their names were probably listed in a book like this somewhere. It is a GREAT blessing that there are men out there like yourself that are here to teach our children to remember where it is we came from. I see from your picture that you are white.
I just wanted to let you know inside your chest must beat the heart of a black man as well, a truly great one as well.

2005-11-16 15:51:13
You Let Him
Excellent write about a terrible problem! i agree with you abuse needs to be stopped. My sister and her children suffered terrible abuse for years and our family had suspicions but couldn't prove anything and he kept them away from us. We have guardianship of my neice and nephew now and my sister is a big part of our lives but she is left with permanent mental problems because of the abuse and he didn't get a thing out of it. The laws need to be tougher. Someone shouldn't have to die before they do something. there are so many deaths at the hands of abuse. It is sad!

2005-11-14 19:44:50
My Greatest Horror
This is simply beyond description. I have never read anything close to being as powerful as this poem. My grandmother lived this. I plan on printing a copy and taking it to her. You are right. If no tells the story everyone will forget. You have done so in a way that will reach the coldest heart and destroy the lies others would try to fabricate forever.

2005-11-03 00:29:42
The Silent Voice
I told one of my friends that i was going to weigh my options. Kate sent me here to read this.
There are choices i have to make, thanks to these words abortion won't be one of them. I guess this is what friends are for and poets as well. Thank you

2005-10-29 00:36:19
5 Single Words
I gave a copy of this poem to my dad yesterday. He cried. It has been hard on him since the hurricane, I was afraid that he might be heading here. I am so glad our teacher had us read your poetry last year. You words are something that stays with you forever. I am sooo glad they were here to help hi as well. thank you for writing this, I'm glad you found the courage to stay here. we need you too.

2005-10-27 17:47:48
A poem written By the Man who left the Bar
DAMN YOU Ed for writing this This quaked me to my very soul I was told by a friend at work to come here and read your poetry This poem made me see myself in these words Everything was going along just fine DAMN YOU for the slap in the face you gave me today Bless you for giving me what I really needed instead I am surprised the word hasn't gotten out about you There are really so many of us that need to hear what you've got to say

2005-10-14 00:28:05
Udomfo Must Die
Sir, in these words you have captured the fragility of the human race and the misfortune which is shared by so many of my people.

I have come to the US to study to try and go back to change things. One of the things i will carry back with me are your words. They shall feed thousands.

2006-12-27 14:53:02

Trying to Understand the Bombing
Dearest Ed, We received notification this last weekend our son was killed in Iraq. His vehicle was hit by a roadside bomb. I had read your poetry here before but saw this poem today for the first time. (Your poem I'll See You Later takes on a new meaning for us) I pray that somehow you can find a way to get this poem to the eyes of those who took my son's life Ed. He was 20, just starting his life. This needs to stop. I truly feel you have the power to do so. Please help!!!!!

2006-12-20 22:08:38
There was a Man
i certainly pray that this wonderful sad truthful poem will make a drinking driver stop and think before they get behind the wheel of a car, which turns into a weapon with a drunk behind the wheel. my heart goes out to you and what you must have had to go through. Take care thank you.

2006-12-19 23:41:43

There was a Man
Extremely powerful write. Having been hit by a drunk driver in my younger days,

I deeply understand the meaning of this poem. Luckily no one was hurt except me with a little whiplash, I was sitting at a red light when the guy plowed into me, I saw him coming and realized he

*wasn't stopping and the intersection was clear so I
tried to pull out of the way but he was driving to fast.
Seemed he wanted the police to arrest me for
scratching his car.*

2006-12-19 23:29:42
Tears of a Soldier
*Very gripping to anyone who has spend a tour on
the battlefields of the world. Excellent, I guess we all
needed something to keep us going through that
horrible time.*

2006-12-15 06:33:24
A Cure for the Past
*Thinking of all your poems I have read today, have
read all of them here, this poem hit home the
hardest. I had a family once, a house, a job, a
purpose in life. I realize I threw it all away in search
of the next buzz, the next high, then just the next
way to escape the one thing I feared the most,
myself. Last week I decided finally to get help. I was
surprised when one of the nurses here
recommended I visit a VERY SPECIAL poetry site.
Of course you know now, that site is yours. This
goes far beyond poetry sir. It is inspiration,
guidance, and most important of all, hope. I'll be
here for awhile then when I leave I will try and build
my life into something , hopefully follow in your
footsteps and give this hope to others.*

Made in the USA
Middletown, DE
30 October 2022

13777048R00156